# Hartmut Wilke

# Turtles

### Everything about Purchase, Care, Nutrition, and Diseases

With 29 Color Photographs by Outstanding Animal
Photographers and 32 Drawings by Fritz W. Köhler

*Translated by* Rita and Robert Kimber

BARRON'S

Woodbury, New York/London/Toronto/Sydney

First English language edition published in 1983 by
Barron's Educational Series, Inc.
© 1979 by Gräfe and Unzer GmbH, Munich, West
Germany.

The title of the German book is *Schildkröten*.

All inquiries should be addressed to:
Barron's Educational Series, Inc.
113 Crossways Park Drive
Woodbury, New York 11797


International Standard Book No. 0-8120-2631-4

Front cover: Common Box Turtle (*Terrapene
carolina carolina*) Size: about 6 inches (15 cm).
Inside front cover: Arrau Turtle (*Podocnemis
expansa*) Size: about 39 inches (100 cm).
Endangered species; also, because of its size,
unsuitable for terrariums.
Inside back cover: European Pond Turtle (*Emys
orbicularis*).
Back cover: Above left: Spotted Turtle (*Clemmys
guttata*). A highly sensitive species and therefore
unsuitable for terrariums. Above right: Juvenile
Red-eared Turtle (*Chrysemys scripta elegans*).
Below left: Painted Turtle (*Chrysemys picta*).
Below right: A soft-shelled species, *Trionyx
steindachneri*.

PRINTED IN HONG KONG
0123    977    15 14 13 12

**Dr. Hartmut Wilke**
Born in Oranienburg in 1943, Dr. Wilke studied
marine biology, hydrobiology, and ichthyology in
Mainz and Hamburg, writing his doctoral
dissertation on diseases of fish. Since 1973, he has
been director of the Exotarium at the Zoological
Gardens in Frankfurt/Main. The Exotarium
houses — along with tropical fish — amphibians,
lizards, snakes, and turtles. Since 1983, he has been
Director of the municipal Darmstadt 200
"Vivarius."

For Barbara and Sebastian

Cover design: Constanze Reithmayr-Frank

*Photo Credits*

Coleman/Bisserot:  Page 9 (below left)
Coleman/Dermid:  Page 64 (below)
Coleman/Fogden:  Back cover (above left)
Coleman/Hirsch:  Page 20 (above left)
Coleman/Plage:  Page 64 (above)
Coleman/Reinhard:  Page 9 (below right)
Hansen:  Page 9 (center left)
König:  Page 63, back cover (above left)
NHPA/Blossom:  Page 9 (above right)
Reinhard:    Page 9 (above left), pages 10, 19, 53,
        front cover, inside front cover, inside
        back cover, back cover (below right)
Schmidecker:  Back cover (below left)
Wicker:  Page 20 (center left and right)
Ziehm:  Page 9 (center right), page 20 (above right,
        below left and right), page 54

# Contents

# Contents

# *Preface*

Dear turtle friend! I am happy to have this opportunity to communicate with you on a subject that is of concern to both of us, namely the proper care of turtles. If turtles are well treated and cared for, they quickly become lovable pets that will learn to recognize you and — with the exception of some species — show this in their trusting attitude toward you. Please bear with me even if the prescriptions for care suggested in this book seem demanding and time-consuming. They are absolutely essential and, for the most part, represent the minimum requirement to insure the survival of your turtle in your home. The most important qualities required of you are careful observation, an ability to imagine what life is like from a turtle's perspective, and, last but not least, intuition, i.e., a sense of what is right in a given situation. If all these elements are present, your pet turtle will be able to live a happy life with you for many years or even decades.

Turtles are among the few creatures that have not changed appreciably in external appearance or way of life since the days of the dinosaurs. That is why we cannot treat them like other pets, such as dogs, cats, or rabbits. This book tries to help you understand turtles in their uniqueness as wild creatures and treat them accordingly. In my work, I see every day how great the need is for guidance in this area. As head of the Exotarium of the Frankfurt Zoo I have gotten innumerable calls and visits from turtle owners with problems, and I have heard many sad tales of turtles that perished not because of ill will on the part of their owners but as a result of sheer ignorance. A study undertaken in 1974 at the Saarland University revealed the shocking fact that about 83 percent of imported turtles die within one year. The causes are stress and injuries sustained during transport, runs that are much too small, and inappropriate environmental conditions. Another reason for the high mortality rate is that turtles are often thoughtlessly given to children who regard them merely as toys or as playmates, which, more often than not, are doomed to an early death. If a turtle dies, this is a harrowing experience for the child, too. In this book, I would like to provide parents with what they need to know to help their children take care of turtles properly. By all means encourage your children to read the book, too!

The proper care of a turtle means that all the basic needs of the wild creature are met. One of the reasons why turtles have survived in an evolutionary process that has stretched over millions of years is that they have specialized in passive self-protection and adapted both body structure and behavior to this end. It is their nature to withdraw into their shell at the slightest sign of danger. If they are jostled or picked up they feel extremely threatened, because in the wild it is usually a predator that does this to them.

The care of turtles requires a selfless love whose reward is simply the pleasure of seeing the animal thrive. That is why turtles should be kept only by responsible people of whatever age who can already give of themselves without expecting anything in return, or who can learn to do so.

Hartmut Wilke

# Considerations Before You Buy

### How to Recognize if a Turtle Is Healthy

• The first thing to find out is whether the turtle of your choice is most active during daylight hours or at dusk. You should then watch it either during the day or in the evening to see if it is moving or swimming around actively and going after bits of food. (The dealer will be happy to arrange a demonstration feeding.)

• If the turtle shows no interest in food, caution is in order. Try again the next day. No properly tended turtle will be so overfed that it will refuse food if it is healthy. If the turtle does not react to food, decide then and there not to buy it.

If your turtle can hold onto your fingers without falling, then it is in good health.

• Next you should check the turtle's general state of health by going over the list of questions on page 6. If even one sign points to illness this is reason enough not to buy.

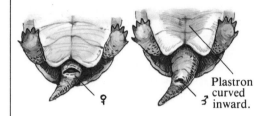

Plastron curved inward.

Sexing turtles. Females: Cloaca near the root of the tail, roots of the tail thin, tail short. Males: Cloaca farther away from the root of the tail, root of the tail thicker, tail somewhat longer. The male's plastron is often markedly concave.

### Determining the Sex

Even experts sometimes cannot answer this question with absolute certainty unless they have observed particular turtles copulating or seen a female lay eggs. It is impossible to positively identify the sex of a young turtle before it reaches sexual maturity. At that point the following guidelines can be applied: In males of many land and water turtles the abdominal shell, or plastron, is more concave than that of the female, the cloaca is located farther down on the tail, and the entire tail is thicker and often considerably longer than in the female.

# *Considerations Before You Buy*

## Size and Life Expectancy

If you buy a young turtle you will want to know how big it will grow in order to plan its future home and figure out the proper dimensions of the terrarium. For detailed information on a turtle's size, turn to the descriptions of the most popular turtle species (pages 13–30). Size also has to be taken into consideration if you intend to keep more than one turtle.

Another factor to give some thought to before actually buying a turtle is how long it is likely to live. Once you acquire a pet—which from that point on is utterly dependent on you for its care—you take on a certain responsibility, and this responsibility may rest on you for a long time indeed. Few people realize that many water turtles as well as land turtles can live to over eighty years.

Within two to three years, a baby land turtle will grow to an adult four times its original size.

## Wintering Over — Hibernation

Some turtles, among them both land and water species from temperate zones, hibernate. You may therefore have to provide an appropriate wintering-over place. Generally, a garden or a cool cellar will do, provided the temperature does not drop below freezing and will not rise above 45°F (7°C) during the period of hibernation.

## Where to Buy a Turtle

The same rule that should be followed no matter what pet you buy applies to turtles, too: Never purchase an animal that you have not had a chance to observe personally. This means, of course, that you cannot buy a turtle *through the mail*. But you can generally find one for much less than a dealer would charge— often for no money at all—by putting *an ad in a newspaper or a pet magazine* (page 73). The best time to do this is a few weeks before summer vacation starts, when many people are at a loss for what to do with their pets. Or you can join one of the societies listed under books and addresses for further help on page 73. These groups periodically publish bulletins which occasionally provide lists of turtles wanted as well as those which are for sale. Taking advantage of this service facilitates the exchange of these turtles, and thus preserves the natural colonies by limiting collecting.

Land turtles. Above: Spur-tailed Mediterranean Land Tortoise *(Testudo hermanni)* and Margined Tortoise *(Testudo marginata)*. Center: Chaco or Argentine Tortoise *(Testudo* [or *Geochelone*] *chilensis)* and Horsfield's Tortoise *(Testudo horsfieldii)*. ▷ Below: Indian Star Tortoise *(Testudo* [or *Geochelone*] *elegans)* and Moorish Tortoise *(Testudo graeca)*.

By following one of these routes you help limit the import of turtles and thus preserve the natural colonies.

No matter where you decide to purchase your turtle, be sure to pick it up yourself. This allows you to watch the turtle's "normal" behavior in its familiar surroundings and assess its state of health, and it gives you a chance to compare notes with the previous owner. If you *buy from a dealer,* check first of all to see if your turtle is on the list of the Washington Convention on International Trade in Endangered Species of Wild Fauna and Flora (pages 71–72). Species listed may not be sold as pets at all. Or you can join one of the societies listed under books and addresses for further help on page 73. These groups periodically publish bulletins which occasionally provide lists of turtles wanted as well as those which are for sale. Taking advantage of this service facilitates the exchange of these turtles, and thus preserves the natural colonies by limiting collecting.

Ask that the full scientific name of your turtle appear on your bill. The dealer is required to supply this information, and this is the only way you can make sure that you are not acquiring a specimen of an endangered species under a false name. Knowing the correct scientific name also makes it easier to consult specialized sources when you want to find information on the habitat, behavior and native climate of your turtle. I also suggest that you look up the turtle you are about to buy in the description of species in this book (pages 13–30). If you do not find it there, it is probably for one of the following reasons:

• The turtle grows too large. (I have described only turtles whose full-grown size is no more than about one foot [30 cm] in length.)
• The turtle belongs to a protected species. (I have restricted the "Descriptions" to species that are not protected by law and that are not mentioned at all in the Washington Convention 1982 edition.)
• The turtle is very expensive to keep. (I have included in the "Descriptions" only turtles whose nutritional and climatic needs can be met at relatively little cost.)

## The Terrarium and Surrounding Conditions

The survival and well-being of a turtle depend to a large extent on how it is housed. A turtle needs a living space where the conditions of its natural habitat prevail, and all aspects of this topic are covered in detail in the chapter on terrariums. You can figure out how large the terrarium has to be as follows: A land turtle needs an area that is in both length and width, about five times the length of the turtle's shell. For a water turtle an area five times as long and three times as wide as the shell is sufficient, assuming an average depth of water of about one foot. Then a little extra should be added to make up for space taken up by the backdrop and decorations. This will amount to about

◁ Mississippi Map Turtle *(Graptemys kohnii)*.
The razor-sharp edges of the beak are clearly
visible in this picture.

thirty percent of the total area if you
plan to simulate a natural background.
You do not have to add anything if you
decide to do without decorations. A last
factor to take into consideration is the
behavior of your particular turtle. It
might be very lively, move and swim
around actively, and therefore need
somewhat more space. Or it might be
very passive, preferring to spend most
of its time hiding in some quiet corner.
In this case there is no allowance necessary for decorations; and, for water
turtles, the original area can even be
reduced to about half. Finally you need
to remember that the members of some
species behave very aggressively toward
their fellows, particularly when they
reach sexual maturity. This is particularly true of males, but it also applies to
the young of many soft-shelled species.
These turtles then have to be housed
singly, even if, according to our calculations, the terrarium should be large
enough for two.

If you intend to keep two or more
turtles, you can apply the following rule
of thumb: Increase the area necessary
for the first turtle by a third for each
additional one. Again there is some
leeway in the case of water turtles, but it
is essential that you allow enough space
for land turtles. Here is an example: A
full-grown land turtle measuring about 8
inches (20 cm) will need a space of 40 ×
40 inches (100 × 100 cm) or about 10
square feet (1 m²). For each additional
turtle, the area has to be increased by
about $3\frac{1}{3}$ square feet. *A terrarium for a
land turtle must never measure less than*

There are always drafts on the floor, even
close to radiators. If you expose your turtle to
cold drafts, it will catch cold and die.

*40 × 20 inches (100 × 50 cm).* These 5
square feet are the bare minimum for a
turtle of 4 to 6 inches (10–15 cm) to survive in and certainly not enough for the
animal to live happily.

Creating the right conditions in the
terrarium is essential. A turtle cannot
produce body heat the way a cat, dog, or
bird can. It is dependent on outside heat
(sunshine) to warm up, and it cools
down by moving into the shade. In this
connection it is important to remember
that even in an airtight room there is
always cool air moving along the floor
due to the air circulation within the
room. If a turtle that has to live on the
floor cools down too much it will inevi-
tably die. A terrarium that is open at the
top and sits on a heated window sill is
just as bad. Particularly in the winter,
cold air moves down from cracks and

11

window panes into the terrarium. Even if the turtle is swimming around in warm water, it will breathe in the cold air — in a process that is barely perceptible to a human observer — and may die of pneumonia or other infectious diseases.

*The first rule, then, is to find a safe spot outside or a raised place indoors away from windows.*

### The Cost of Keeping Turtles

**Terrarium:** A high quality, commercially available terrarium measuring about 48 × 20 × 24 inches (120 × 50 × 60 cm) costs around $150. An aquarium of similar dimensions for water or marsh turtles is similar in price, and an aqua-terrarium with enough space for decorations will come to about $250 (prices figured as of 1983). In addition you may need a small quarantine terrarium for cases of illness (page 37). The cost will be considerably less if you build the terrarium yourself, but be sure not to skimp on materials.

**Food:** Hardly any turtles are either pure vegetarians or pure carnivores, and their varied basic diet has to be supplemented by additions of either meat or vegetable foods (page 45). A one-sided diet can, in the long run, result in your pet's death. The cost of commercial dry food supplemented with fresh treats comes to between five and ten dollars per month for one to three full-grown turtles.

**Water:** If water and marsh turtles are to thrive it is essential that the water, which is, after all, the element they spend most of their life in, be of excellent quality. Depending on the size and arrangement of the terrarium (page 31), a full-grown turtle requires approximately 125 to 500 gallons of water (500 to 2000 liters) per month, which may cost up to two dollars.

**Electricity:** The water always has to be heated, and it takes a thermostatically controlled heater of 250 to 300 watts to heat 50 gallons (200 liters) of water. Just how much electricity this will take is hard to predict, because it depends on the type of terrarium you have and on the room temperature. Heat lamps also run on electricity (page 32). If you run a heat lamp of 60 to 300 watts eight to twelve hours daily, it will use up about .5 to 3.6 kW/h per day. Finally there is the electric filter and water pump, but at 35 to 50 watts the cost of running it, even around the clock, is negligible.

Once you have taken all these points into consideration and concluded that you are able to provide a turtle with enough space and food, that you are willing to spend the necessary money on technical apparatus and electricity, and that you are prepared to look after a turtle for several decades if necessary, then you have met all the prerequisites for owning a turtle and are now ready to decide what kind of turtle you would like to have.

# The Most Important Land and Water Turtles

## Explanation of the Descriptions

In the biological classification system, all land turtles are assigned to one family. The same is not true of water turtles. There is no scientific class or family that includes all water turtles. In this book I have used a simplified system and included under the heading "water turtles" all those turtles that live primarily in water, no matter what family they belong to. This category takes in, among others, mud turtles, soft-shelled turtles, side-necked and snake-necked turtles. Under the descriptions of the individual species, you will find both scientific and common names, size, and information on the biology, habitat, environmental needs, and behavior of different turtles, as well as everything you need to know about feeding and wintering over.

**Names:** The scientific name of an animal is made up of two, occasionally three, parts. The scientific "first name" indicates the genus, the "last name" the species of the animal. For example: *Testudo* is the genus, *elegans* the species. Sometimes you will find a name made up of three words, as in *Chrysemys scripta elegans* and *Chrysemys scripta scripta*. These two subspecies differ somewhat from each other, but they are still similar enough for individuals to crossbreed over several generations. This is impossible once two species have become distinct. Following the scientific term, the name of the scientist who first studied and described the turtle is given in capital letters.

**Size and Special Biological Information:** The size given indicates the average length of a full-grown turtle. In addition to a short sketch of the turtle's biology, this section includes various facts characteristic of the particular species.

**Habitat:** Here you will find information on where the turtle occurs in the wild. You will get a picture of its natural surroundings, learn whether it needs sandy or clayey ground to dig in, low bushes for cover, caves as hiding places, or lots of room to move around in.

**Environmental Needs:** Here you find out what the climate is like in the turtle's natural habitat. These descriptions will help you determine how you should vary temperature, humidity, and food in the course of the year. You will also want to know whether the difference between daytime and nighttime temperatures is significant or negligible. The lower number gives the lowest reading to which night-time temperatures drop. The higher number indicates the *average* of the higher temperature readings during the day. You should measure this temperature in an open, shady area, waving the thermometer back and forth rapidly. You should also note here whether the turtle is used to high humidity or to a dry climate.

**Behavior:** Knowledge about a given species' behavior is important for arranging the bottom and the backdrop of the terrarium. Whether a turtle likes to dig or not, for instance, determines how deep or shallow the bottom material should be. Or, if it likes to move about a lot, you will want to incorporate generous uncluttered areas in the bottom.

If I describe certain turtles as "sociable" or "good-natured," this is meant in a limited sense. First of all, this

# The Most Important Land and Water Turtles

characterization usually applies only to young animals. As I have already mentioned, turtles acquire territorial habits when they reach sexual maturity. This territoriality can be more or less developed and is usually more pronounced in water turtles than land-dwelling ones. *That is why mature water turtles of the same sex and species must be kept singly.* (No indoor terrarium could possibly be large enough to contain two separate territories.)

Secondly, it is indeed possible to crowd two grown turtles together in too small a terrarium for a short period without their attacking each other. This is true because turtles kept in too confined a space give up their territorial behavior. But this lies completely outside the kind of biologically adequate conditions we seek to encourage and strive to achieve. Keeping turtles in such a situation is outright cruelty to animals.

Water turtles sunbathing on a log. If there is not enough room, turtles will often climb on top of each other.

Thirdly, you might say that in nature large gatherings of fully grown turtles are common, as on sunny beaches, for instance. But in contrast to the captives in a terrarium, these "sun worshippers" always have plenty of room to get out of the way in case a neighbor begins to assert territorial claims. For all these reasons we have to make the cautious assumption—no matter whether a particular turtle is described as relatively good-natured or not—that sooner or later our turtles will exhibit territorial behavior.

**Food:** Here you will find brief mention of the kinds of food specific species of turtles eat; how to compose a turtle's menu is discussed more fully elsewhere (pages 45–47).

**Hibernation:** As in the case of "Food," wintering over is discussed in greater detail elsewhere.

# The Most Important Land and Water Turtles

## Descriptions of Land Turtles

### Spur-Tailed Mediterranean Tortoise

*Testudo hermanni* GMELIN
Color picture, page 9.

This tortoise inhabits an area that includes not only Greece but also the Balkan peninsula and extends as far as the Danube. (The terms *turtle, tortoise,* and *terrapin* are all in common use. Although some writers use *turtle* and *tortoise* for fresh-water species, it is more common to restrict *tortoise* to animals which live only on land. *Terrapin* is a loose term for certain American fresh-water turtles, especially those used as food by man. It would be accurate to refer to all of these reptiles with shells as *turtles*. In Great Britain the term *tortoise* is used to refer to any non-marine turtle.) This tortoise is also found in southern Italy, but this strain is regarded as a subspecies *(Testudo hermanni hermanni)*. A second subspecies *(Testudo hermanni robertmertensi)* inhabits central Italy and areas on the northwestern Mediterranean: Corsica, Sardinia, the Balearic islands, southern France, and eastern Spain.
**Size:** Up to about 8 inches (20 cm)
**Habitat:** Open, steppe-like ground with some rocks and shrubbery; much sunshine and light shady areas.
**Environmental Needs:** Subtropical (Mediterranean) climate, i.e., warm, with dry summers.

We should keep these tortoises outdoors as much as possible during the summer, but only if the air temperature does not drop below ca. 65°F (18°–19°C) at night and rises to about 83° to 86°F (28°–30°C) during the day. In the spring and fall, we have to keep the temperature in the terrarium at these levels.
**Behavior:** These tortoises are active during the day; they are good climbers and diggers and are very lively if kept properly.
**Food:** Both plant and animal.
**Hibernation:** Yes.

### Spur-Thighed Mediterranean Land Tortoise

*Testudo graeca* LINNÉ
Color picture, page 9.

This species can be subdivided according to its geographical distribution into four subspecies. It occurs in southern Europe as well as in Iran, Egypt, Libya, and Morocco.
**Size:** May grow larger than 12 inches (30 cm).
**Habitat:** Open, steppe-like ground, as described above for Spur-Tailed Mediterranean Tortoise.
**Environmental Needs:** The Moorish Tortoise is found wherever subtropical conditions prevail (warm, dry summer, "Mediterranean" climate). Temperature: 65°–83°F (18°–28°C).
**Behavior:** Active during the day, likes to climb and dig.
**Food:** Both plant and animal.
**Hibernation:** Yes.

# The Most Important Land and Water Turtles

## Margined Spur-thighed Mediterranean Land Tortoise

*Testudo marginata* SCHOEPFF
Color picture, page 9.

This is the third and last of the truly "European" land turtles. Its natural area of distribution is rather small and consists only of southern Greece. (It is also found on Sardinia, where it was introduced at some time in the past.) In striking contrast to the other two European species, the Margined Tortoise has a carapace with an elongated posterior margin. This creates something like an awning that shades the hind legs when the tortoise walks.

**Size:** Up to about 12 inches (30 cm).
**Habitat:** Sunny, wind-still slopes covered with thick grass and shrubbery through which the tortoise makes narrow paths.
**Environmental Needs:** The same as for Spur-tailed Mediterranean Land Tortoise.
**Behavior:** Active during the day; good at climbing and digging.
**Food:** Both plant and animal.
**Hibernation:** Yes.

## Horsfield's Tortoise

*Testudo (Agrionemys) horsfieldii* GRAY
Color picture, page 9.

This tortoise lives east of the Caspian Sea and from Iran to Pakistan. It is adapted to the subtropical and desert climates that predominate there with hot dry summers and, in the subtropical regions, warm and dry or, in mountain regions, harsh winters. In the wild this tortoise restricts its activity largely to those months when the climate is tolerable and food available. It spends the rest of the time — cold winters (as well as cold nights) and desiccating heat periods — sleeping in burrows up to 36 feet (12 meters) long. The additional "dry sleep" in the summer is probably not as crucial for the well-being of the tortoise as hibernation but is a means to avoid dying of hunger or thirst. It also seems to coordinate the readiness to mate, i.e., it assures that the tortoises are willing to engage in sexual activity at the same time. The egg laying (in July) is timed in such a way that the development of the embryo is slowed in the summer and winter and extends over eight months, so that the young do not hatch until April, the month with the greatest rainfall when there is plenty of food available. This tortoise has only four toes per foot.

**Size:** Up to about 8 inches (20 cm).
**Habitat:** Dry, fairly flat steppes with sandy to clayey soil; sparse growth of grass and shrubs; lush only in the spring.
**Environmental Needs:** As above. Keep this tortoise outdoors during the summer, and keep it supplied with food.
**Temperature:** 65°–85°F (18°–30°C).
**Behavior:** Lively, active during the day, good-natured; likes to dig and should have deep, solidly packed soil (8–12 inches [20 – 30 cm]) or ready-made caves in the terrarium.
**Food:** Both plant and animal.
**Hibernation:** Yes.

# The Most Important Land and Water Turtles

**Argentine Tortoise** or **Chaco Tortoise**

*Testudo (chelonoides) chilensis* GRAY
Color picture, page 9.

This tortoise is not native to Chile, as the scientific name would seem to indicate, but to Argentina and Uruguay. It has a steep, flat facial profile, due primarily to the elongated tip of the upper beak that juts down over the lower mandible (do not file off this tip!).

**Size:** Up to about 8 inches (20 cm).

**Habitat:** This tortoise prefers rather dry surroundings and lives in the moderately fertile regions of Uruguay (grown over with grass, other greens, and shrubs) as well as in the meager steppes of Argentina that are covered with tough grasses and thorny bushes.

**Environmental Needs:** Their native habitat includes regions of subtropical climate (warm summers, mild winters, plenty of rainfall throughout the year) and areas of harsher conditions (warm summers and cold winters with not much precipitation). Temperature: 68° to 82°F (20°–28°C). "Variable" precipitation. This tortoise can be kept in the garden during the summer.

**Behavior:** Active during the day, good-natured.

**Food:** Both plant and animal.

**Hibernation:** No.

**Star Tortoise**

*Testudo* (or *Geochelone*) *elegans*
SCHOEPFF
Color picture, page 9.

The striking yellowish star-shaped design against a dark, blackish-brown ground on the carapace makes this a very attractive-looking tortoise. Unfortunately it is, like the Box Turtle, very sensitive and rarely survives for more than a few years even in the hands of a very experienced keeper. Probably this tortoise needs very specific climatic conditions and/or food of a certain kind, needs that we do not as yet understand and cannot therefore meet in the captive's environment. For this reason I cannot recommend buying an Indian Star Tortoise. The information given here is included only to facilitate the best possible care, as far as that can be determined in the light of present knowledge, for those tortoises that are already living in captivity.

**Size:** Up to about 10 inches (25 cm).

**Habitat:** In its native India and Sri Lanka (Ceylon), this tortoise prefers sandy steppes with scattered rocks and a sparse growth of grass, shrubs, and other plants. It likes to hide in cave-like nooks and hollows.

**Environmental Needs:** Tropical grasslands make up this tortoise's native range which is characterized by humid heat in the summer and cold in the winter. Because it is used to wet summers, this tortoise needs not only a high air humidity (above 70%) but also plenty of

17

Above: A male Caspian Turtle *(Clemmys* [or ▷ *Mauremys] caspica rivulata).* Below: Common Musk Turtle *(Sternotherus odoratus).*

water for drinking and bathing (one drinking bowl will not do). Temperature: 72° to 82°F (22°–28°C).
**Behavior:** In the wild, this tortoise is active only during the cooler evening hours, but in captivity it will go foraging in the morning as well. It spends the days hidden away, a protective measure against overheating.
**Food:** Feeds on both plants and animals but with a large emphasis on plants (90%).
**Hibernation:** No.

## Ornate Box Turtle

*Terrapene ornata* AGASSIZ

In terms of environmental adaptation, this turtle is on the borderline between land and water turtles. (Scientists include all *Terrapene* species in the family of marsh turtles. Consequently, the Ornate Box Turtle is, strictly speaking, a marsh turtle that has adapted to a relatively dry habitat.)

This turtle, like all box turtles, has a hinge running horizontally across the middle of the plastron, which considerably improves the protective function of the shell. If the turtle is attacked, it can draw the front and back ends of the lower shell up against the edge of the carapace, thus creating a tight "box" without any openings. The iris of the mature male is reddish, while that of the female is yellowish-brown.

I want to point out here that even very knowledgeable turtle fanciers have thus far not had very good luck in keeping Ornate Box Turtles. Since it is not clear in what way their care failed, I strongly advise you to stay away from this species. I have included it here only in the hope of preventing major mistakes in the care of animals already held in captivity. The Common Box Turtle (color picture on front cover), which is even more difficult to keep, is a close relative of the Ornate Box Turtle.
**Size:** Up to 6 inches (15 cm).
**Habitat:** Broadly speaking, the areas around the western tributaries of the Mississippi, with the western mountain ranges acting as a border. The turtles are found on grasslands, on fertile plains with some light brush, and on sandy, half dry soils near bodies of water.
**Environmental Needs:** Fairly dry habitat. These turtles are adapted both to the climate of grasslands (warm, moderately wet summers and cold, dry winters) and to more tropical conditions, characterized by warm or hot summers, mild winters, and high precipitation throughout the year. Temperature: 65° to 82°F (18°–28°C).

Ornate Box Turtles can be kept outdoors during the summer. If they are kept in the terrarium, make sure to supply "morning and evening sun."
**Behavior:** Unlike the species described so far, these turtles are active only in the morning and evening. They are fairly lively and peaceable. During the day they like to hide.
**Food:** Both plants and meat, with a strong preference for meat.
**Hibernation:** Yes.

18

◁ Marsh and water turtles that are easy to keep. Above: Caspian Turtle *(Clemmys* [or *Mauremys] caspica rivulata)* and River Cooter *(Chrysemys concina).* Center: Chinese Soft-shelled Turtle *(Trionyx sinensis)* and a common snake-necked turtle, *Chelodina longicollis.* Below: Malayan Box Turtle *(Cuora amboinensis)* and *Siebenrockiella crassicollis.*

Apparently a sudden increase in the moisture of the soil plays an important role in rousing these turtles from hibernation. In April or May you should water the packing material in the wintering-over box with a watering can and at the same time raise the surrounding temperature to about 80°F (26°C). The turtle can then remain in the box "half awake" for up to two weeks before emerging to active life.

# Descriptions of Marsh and Water Turtles

## Caspian Terrapin

(1) *Clemmys* (or *Mauremys*) *caspica caspica* GMELIN

This subspecies of Caspian turtle inhabits the countries that border on the southern half of the Caspian Sea, favoring the flatter low-lying regions. This means that its native waters are slow-moving and warm. The scientific name indicates that this is a subspecies. There are two others, which will be discussed next.

**Size:** Up to about 10 inches (25 cm).
**Habitat:** Sunny, flat brooks, rivers, and lakes in plains and broad valleys. The turtles like to sunbathe on shores with large loose rocks, bushes, and ground vegetation.
**Environmental Needs:** These turtles are found both in zones that have central European conditions (moderately warm summers, rain throughout the year) and in subtropical climates (warm all year, dry summers). Winters are generally mild.

Water and air temperatures: 72° to 82°F (20°–28°C) from spring to fall. If the turtle gives no indication of wanting to hibernate, these temperatures are maintained during the winter as well. Can be kept outdoors in the summer.
**Behavior:** This turtle is quite lively and likes to climb. It defends its favorite spot (its territory) against intruders. If you keep more than one turtle, you have to allow plenty of space and make sure to follow our rule of thumb for determining the size of the aquarium. These turtles are active during the day.
**Food:** Plant and animal, with a strong emphasis on meat.
**Hibernation:** Yes and no. Only careful observation in the late fall will give you a clear answer (page 42).

(2) *Clemmys* (or *Mauremys*) *caspica rivulata* VALENCIENNES
Color picture, pages 19 and 20.

This subspecies is a geographical neighbor of the one we have just discussed, separated from it by Anatolia and the Taurus mountains which offer no adequate habitat to either subspecies. *C.* (or *M.*) *caspica rivulata* occurs in all the Mediterranean countries from Israel in the South to Bulgaria in the East and Yugoslavia in the North, as well as on most of the Greek islands.
**Size:** Up to about 8 inches (20 cm).
**Habitat:** The same as for *C.* (or *M.*) *caspica caspica* except that this turtle

# The Most Important Land and Water Turtles

also likes dense reed growths.
**Environmental Needs:** The same as above.
**Behavior:** These turtles climb well, like to spend time on land, and exhibit strongly territorial behavior. They are active during the day.
**Food:** Plant and animal, with emphasis on meat.
**Hibernation:** Yes and no as above.

(3) *Clemmys* (or *Mauremys*) *caspica leprosa* SCHWEIGGER
This subspecies occurs mostly in western Europe. It is found in Spain, Portugal, and, on the African continent, along the rivers of Algeria.
**Size:** Up to about 10 inches (25 cm).
**Habitat:** Slow-moving streams and rivers, ponds and lakes, often with rocky shores.
**Environmental Needs:** These turtles live in regions with hot dry summers and mild winters (Mediterranean climate) as well as in climates characteristic of steppes (hot summers, warm winters). They are therefore used to higher air and water temperatures (ca. 72° to 85°F [22°–30°C]) than the two other subspecies and should be kept outdoors only in the heat of summer.
**Behavior:** This subspecies is markedly territorial, which has to be taken into consideration if more than one turtle is kept. Being excellent climbers, these turtles have been observed making their way down almost vertical rocky slopes head first. They are active during the day.

**Food:** Plant and animal, with a strong preference for meat.
**Hibernation:** Yes and no, as above.

**European Pond Turtle**

*Emys orbicularis* LINNÉ
Color picture, inside back cover.
This is the only turtle native to Germany, and its survival there is threatened because the draining of wet areas keeps diminishing its habitat year by year. This is why it has been placed under legal protection that forbids trade in turtles captured in Germany. This is the last in our list of native European turtles.
European Pond Turtles all have paired extensions of the cloaca (anal bladder) that reach way into the body and can, if needed, be filled with water. These "water bags" are thought to function in part as an auxiliary breathing organ or internal "gills," to help maintain the proper balance between body and water while swimming, and to serve as water storage for moistening the eggs. Not all water turtles have this physiological characteristic. You can easily test whether a given turtle has water bags or not. Pick it up and see if it sprays water.
**Size:** Up to about 10 inches (25 cm).
**Habitat:** European Pond Turtles are found all over the European continent up to the 55th degree of latitude. Their range ends in the east at the line running from Finland down along the Volga to the Caspian Sea, and it extends as far

south as Anatolia, Greece, Sicily, and Algeria. This turtle prefers swamps of all kinds, stands of alders, still lakes, ponds, and ditches that are weeded over, and likes to spend time on shore among not too dense bushes or rocks.

**Environmental Needs:** Being at home in a temperate climate, this turtle is easy to keep outdoors; keeping it exclusively indoors can, in fact, lead to a general deterioration of health. Water and air temperature: 68° to 82°F (20°–28°C).

**Behavior:** This turtle is territorial, lively, and climbs well. It is active during the day.

**Food:** Plant and animal, with a marked preference for meat.

**Hibernation:** Yes.

## Mississippi Map Turtle

*Graptemys kohnii* BAUR
Color picture, page 10.

In the young of this species, there are humps along the midline of the carapace. The young also have brightly colored markings on their backs that fade with age. Map Turtles do not tolerate radical changes of their original living conditions well and are therefore not ideal for beginning turtle keepers.

**Size:** Up to about 10 inches (25 cm).

**Habitat:** This turtle inhabits the southern United States. It is found in the fertile plains along the lower Mississippi and its tributaries and as far north as the lower Missouri. It likes still, small, and

weedy bodies of water with plenty of shore growth and water creatures (insects, fish). It prefers sunning on driftwood rather than on dry land, and we should therefore provide it with a floating island.

**Environmental Needs:** Its exclusive preference for the southern states implies that this species prefers a warm climate. And, in fact, the summers are hot where this turtle ranges, and it likes to spend its time on sunny shores and in water of 72° to 82°F (22°–28°C). Air temperature: 72° to 82°F (22°–28°C). To be kept outdoors only on sunny, hot summer days.

**Behavior:** Little is known about this turtle's behavior in the wild. Active during the day.

**Food:** Plant and animal, with a preference for meat.

**Hibernation:** Yes.

## False Map Turtle

*Graptemys pseudogeographica* GRAY

There are four subspecies of this turtle that are distinguished from each other by the different markings on the face. There is no need here to give individual descriptions. It is important, however, to know that the four subspecies have different and only partially overlapping ranges, some more northerly and some more southerly, and are thus used to different climates. In order to provide proper care you have to find out where your turtle comes from. This turtle, too,

should be kept only by experienced hob-
byists who are able to recognize and
meet its specific needs.

**Size:** Up to about 10 inches (25 cm).

**Habitat:** The entire area near the
Mississippi and its tributaries, as well as
Texas. The False Map Turtle prefers
small bodies of water rich in vegetation,
though it occurs also in clear, fast-
moving streams. It likes to spend most
of its time in the water. Like the
Mississippi Map Turtle, it favors driftwood rather than land for basking in the
sun, and we should therefore equip the
terrarium with a floating island rather
than a strip of sand.

**Environmental Needs:** Depending on the
subspecies it belongs to, this turtle likes
warm summers and cold winters (northern US) or hot summers and mild
winters (southern US). All the subspecies
love sunshine. Air and water temperature: 68° to 82°F (20°–28°C) for northern subspecies; 72° to 82°F (22°–28°C)
for southern subspecies. These turtles
seem to be very sensitive to lower temperatures and should therefore be kept
outdoors only during very hot weather.
They like to have resting spots with
plenty of light.

**Behavior:** Very lively when young;
sedate and rather shy when mature; active during the day.

**Food:** Animal and plant (including
aquatic plants), with a clear preference
for meat.

**Hibernation:** Yes, if breeding is to occur.

## Red-eared Turtle

*Chrysemys scripta elegans* WIED
Color pictures, page 53 and back
cover.


and

## Cumberland Turtle

*Chrysemys scripta troosti* HOLBROOK

The Red-eared Turtle is the only
species that is bred in large numbers spe-
cifically and for the pet trade. It is the
only turtle that can be recommended —
within limits — for a novice. The process
of learning to keep turtles may otherwise
cost the lives of turtles captured in the
wild.

**Caution:** There are two other species
that, to the layman, will look like the
Red-eared Turtle, namely the Cooter, *C.
floridana* and the River Cooter, *C. con-
cinna* (color picture, page 20), both of
which grow up to 16 inches (40 cm) long
and develop a carapace nearly 8 inches
(20 cm) high.

I am discussing only two members of
the *Chrysemys* genus in order not to con-
fuse the reader utterly. There are so
many sub-divisions of this genus (at least
ten species split up into at least thirty-
one subspecies) that a brief survey would
be more bewildering than enlightening.
A positive identification — if a layman
wants to attempt one at all — can be
made only on the basis of young animals
because the markings, on which such
identification can be based, largely

# The Most Important Land and Water Turtles

disappear with age. The two subspecies I mention here are the ones you are most likely to encounter.

When they are still young, about the size of a half dollar, and brightly colored, the two subspecies can be distinguished from each other by the colored stripe that runs along the temples, a stripe that is red in the Red-eared Turtle and bright yellow in the Cumberland Turtle.

**Size:** Up to about 10 inches (25 cm).

**Habitat:** Central United States. The Red-eared Turtle is found both east and west of the Mississippi, the Cumberland Turtle only in spots east of the Mississippi. Both like slow-moving, soft-bottomed, weedy waters of all kinds that warm up with the sun and have flat, sunny shores.

**Environmental Needs:** Warm to hot summers, mild winters, lots of sun, warm water. Can be kept outdoors in the summer. Water and air temperature: 68° to 90°F (20°–32°C).

**Behavior:** These turtles are *not* sociable but seem rather solitary in nature. In the height of summer their activity may temporarily slow down and their food intake decrease for a month or two. They should revive fully for one to two months before settling down for hibernation in October. They are lively, active during the day, and spend most of their time in the water.

**Food:** Both plant and animal; young turtles prefer meat (70% meat, 30% plant); grown ones mostly plants (90% plant, 10% meat).

**Hibernation:** Yes.

## Painted Turtle

*Chrysemys picta* SCHNEIDER
Color picture, back cover.

This species, which is characterized by yellow and red stripes on the head and legs, is subdivided into four subspecies which are distinguished from each other by the coloration of the plastron and the arrangement of the scutes on the carapace. Study of this species has shown that sexual maturity in turtles depends less on age than on physical size. Females have to be 4 inches (10 cm) long to become sexually mature, males about $3\frac{1}{4}$ to $3\frac{1}{2}$ inches (8–9 cm). Assuming normal growth, these turtles reach those sizes when they are about five years old. Their average life expectancy in the wild is about ten to twenty years.

**Size:** Up to 10 inches (25 cm).

**Habitat:** One or more of the subspecies are found in almost all of the states east of the Mississippi and throughout the northern part of the U.S. west of the Mississippi. Painted turtles are absent only in the great deserts and rugged mountain ranges of the Southwest. Their preferred habitat is slow, weedy waters where they forage for food along the bottom as well as on the surface. Large pieces of driftwood are favorite places for basking in the sun. (Supply a floating island in the terrarium!)

**Environmental Needs:** Since this species is so widely distributed over large parts of the U.S., individual turtles may come from varied climates. It is very useful to know where a particular turtle was col-

# The Most Important Land and Water Turtles

lected, but in general this species can adapt to a relatively radical change in temperature. The temperature in the terrarium should lie between 68° and 77°F (20°–25°C), and the turtles should always be given the opportunity of sunbathing and reaching a body temperature of about 77°F (25°C).

**Behavior:** This turtle, which is active during the day, spends its time alternating, usually about every hour, between foraging for food and basking in the sun. It likes bright, warm spots and stays away from fast-moving water.

**Food:** About half meat and half plant. These turtles also feed at the water's surface, sucking in algae, mosquitoes, fish eggs, and insects between opened jaws with a pumping motion of the floor of the mouth.

**Hibernation:** Yes, at the bottom of deeper and darker stretches of water at about 43°F (6°C).

## Common Musk Turtle

*Sternotherus odoratus* LATREILLE
Color picture, page 19.

The carapace of this species is rounded and has a slight keel. If the turtle is bothered, it can emit an unpleasant odor, which gives this turtle its name.

**Size:** Up to about 6 inches (15 cm).

**Habitat:** This is the most widely distributed North American turtle described here, ranging from Canada north of the Great Lakes to Florida, as well as being found in Texas. Like the Painted Turtle, the Musk Turtle likes to hide in the dim reaches at the bottom of deep waters.

**Environmental Needs:** Because of the wide distribution of this species, individual turtles may have different needs. A turtle from the north can be kept in an outdoor terrarium in temperate zones, which would be quite inappropriate for a turtle from the subtropical climate of Florida. Such a turtle should be outside only in hot weather. Common Musk Turtles do not seem to need sun baths; at least they have never been observed basking in the sun in the wild. Air and water temperature: 68° to 77°F (20°–25°C) for those from the north; 74° to 82°F (23°–28°C) for those from the south.

**Behavior:** This species is active both at night and during the day, generally fairly quiet, but quite aggressive when foraging for food.

**Food:** Omnivorous but with a strong emphasis on meat (90%).

**Hibernation:** Yes and no; here, too, only careful observation in the fall can help you decide, particularly if you do not know exactly where the turtle was collected.

## Mud Turtle

*Kinosternon subrubrum* LACÉPÈDE

There are three subspecies of this turtle that I do not want to describe separately in this book but that can be identified with the help of the appropriate literature. It is easier to tell the sexes apart since the males have longer and more curved claws on the forelegs than the females. Also, the tail of the male — but not that of the female — terminates in a horny nail. Mud Turtles reach sexual maturity when they are from 3 to $4\frac{1}{4}$ inches (8–12 cm) long. The male reaches this length at an age of 4 to 7, the female at 5 to 8 years. Like the closely related Musk Turtle, the Mud Turtle can flip movable parts of the plastron up and close off the openings at the front and back of its shell.

**Size:** Up to about $4\frac{1}{2}$ inches (12 cm).

**Habitat:** This turtle is found on the plains along the Mississippi and its tributaries as well as along the entire eastern seaboard of the U.S. It prefers still, weedy water from which it can climb on land or breathe without having to make use of its rather limited swimming abilities. This turtle therefore needs fair-sized landed areas that slope gently into the water (divide the terrarium into half landed area and half water).

**Environmental Needs:** The range of this turtle includes both warm and cool climates. In the wild, it prefers water of about 75°F (23°–24°C) and is most active at air temperatures between 72° and 80°F (22°–27°C), developing a body temperature of up to 94°F (34°C).

**Behavior:** Activity varies during the day. In the morning and evening, this turtle forages for food vigorously. The rest of the time is spent quietly at the bottom of the water, in caves, under tree roots, or bathing among submerged bushes. Individual turtles behave very differently from each other; some bite, others are good-natured. I cannot therefore recommend keeping a Mud Turtle together with other turtles or with another member of its own species.

**Food:** Young turtles of less than 2 inches (5 cm) diameter live mainly on water insects and their larvae as well as aquatic vegetation (in the terrarium substitute tender lettuce leaves and other greens). Older turtles will eat anything that falls in the water, including meat from larger mammals. Give your turtle meat and vegetarian food in roughly equal parts.

**Hibernation:** Yes and no. In the wild, Mud Turtles living in a colder climate winter burrowed in the ground either on shore or in the water; those living in the south are active throughout the year. If your turtle gives no indication of wanting to hibernate, there is no reason to worry (page 44).

## Indian Roof Turtle

*Kachuga smithii* GRAY
First of all, let me say that since 1977 Indian turtles, like the one I mention here, can be exported only with a permit from the Indian government. A close relative of this species, the *K. tecta tecta,* is in danger of extinction and therefore listed in Appendix I of the Washington Convention. Thus, it is particularly important to have papers proving that your turtle was legally exported.

**Size:** Up to about 10 inches (25 cm).

**Habitat:** This species inhabits the Indus and the Ganges, including all their tributaries, favoring deep, clear, slightly moving waters.

**Environmental Needs:** The range of this species is subject to varied but hot climates characterizing deserts, steppes, and savannas. Consequently the air and water temperature for these turtles should be 74° to 95°F (23°–29°C) all year round.

**Behavior:** These turtles are usually peaceable and active during the day. Except for laying their eggs, they normally do not go on land but spend all their time in the water. A floating island that is covered with earth for egg laying is all the land that is needed.

**Food:** Meat and plant, with a strong preference for the latter (90%).

**Hibernation:** No.

### Amboina Box Turtle

*Cuora amboinensis* DAUDIN
Color picture, page 20.

The young of this species are characterized by three longitudinal keels on their brown carapaces. With age this striking feature disappears. The second characteristic, which is reflected in the turtle's name, remains: a plastral hinge that allows the shell to be closed up tightly and that insures the same protection we encounter in the American box turtles. (This should give you some idea of how sensible this invention is for survival. Nature invented it twice on two separate continents and preserved it, among hundreds of other possibilities, as

the most useful to survival.)

**Size:** Up to about 8 inches (20 cm).

**Habitat:** Found throughout Southeast Asia, this turtle likes very slow-moving and preferably still waters that make no great demands on its swimming abilities.

**Environmental Needs:** Its native habitat is subject to hot, wet summers and warm to hot winters (the climate of tropical rain forests and savannas). We should therefore keep it year round in water 75° to 86°F (24°–30°C) and in comparable air temperatures. If water or air temperatures drop even briefly below 65°F (18°C), the danger of harmful effects is great.

**Behavior:** Active during the day, these turtles are relatively agreeable. Since some individuals do not like to swim, the depth of the water should be such that they can rest in certain places, as on submerged stones.

**Food:** Both plant and meat.

**Hibernation:** No.

### Emydid Turtle (family)

*Siebenrockiella crassicollis* GRAY
Color picture, page 20.

This turtle is imported in relatively large numbers, but not much is known about its habits. Because of the upturned ends of its mouth, it seems to be perpetually smiling, but this is not necessarily an indication of a friendly disposition. To be on the safe side, I would recommend keeping this turtle singly.

**Size:** Up to about 8 inches (20 cm).

# The Most Important Land and Water Turtles

**Habitat:** This species is found throughout Southeast Asia and lives in ponds and sluggish water.

**Environmental Needs:** This turtle comes from tropical forests and savannas where the summers are hot and humid and the winters warm. It should be kept in water and air temperatures of 74° to 86°F (24°-30°C).

**Behavior:** These turtles are of a relatively quiescent nature, which can be observed both in their foraging behavior and their limited need for exercise. They move about the bottom of the water, swim around a bit, and rest on the shore.

**Food:** This turtle is omnivorous, feeding on water creatures as well as on fruit, greens, and aquatic plants of all kinds.

**Hibernation:** No.

## Chinese Soft-shelled Turtle

*Trionyx sinensis* WIEGMANN
Color picture, page 20.

This turtle lacks an external horny layer on the shell. Instead, the bony parts of the shell are covered with a soft but tough and leathery skin, which offers nowhere as much protection as a solid shell does. On the other hand, this skin serves well as a kind of lung, relieving the lung proper of up to 70% of the job of breathing.

**Size:** Up to about 10 inches (25 cm).

**Habitat:** This turtle is found in eastern Asia from the Amur river in the north down to Indochina in the south, and it also occurs in Hawaii. Living in still to slowly moving waters, it likes to settle into the mud in shallow areas where it can take in air without exerting itself. We have to arrange the water depth in the terrarium accordingly, and we have to supply "substitute mud" in the shape of very fine river silt about the consistency of flour and without sharp edges. It must not, therefore, be artificially ground to size.

**Environmental Needs:** Since the climate varies widely with the north-south distribution of this turtle, it is important to know the site where your turtle was caught. Water and air temperatures from 72° to 86°F (22°-30°C) will probably be adequate since import from the northern part of its range, the Chinese Republic, is not likely.

**Behavior:** This turtle spends most of its time peacefully resting in the mud and occasionally raising its nostrils above water to take a breath. It goes on land only to lay eggs. Active during the day and mean, it may attack its keeper. Even young turtles will bite each other to death. Except at mating time, Chinese Soft-shells must therefore be kept singly.

**Food:** Both meat and plant, with a clear preference for meat (90%).

**Hibernation:** No, except for turtles from the northernmost areas, i.e., China. These require hibernation.

**Special Care:** Faulty care, such as polluted water or shell injuries from rough rocks, will allow fungi to establish themselves on the shell and lead to the turtle's death because they cannot be removed. Since this species often lives in

# The Most Important Land and Water Turtles

brackish rivers, you can try to treat an infected turtle with a solution of sea water of 20% to 25% salinity ( = about $\frac{3}{4}$ oz. of table salt per 2 quarts of water [20–25 grams per liter]). A solution of this strength kills many fungi within two to three weeks. If this is not effective consult a veterinarian for treatment.

## Snake-necked Turtle

*Chelodina longicollis* SHAW
Color picture, page 20.

This turtle differs from all the other turtles discussed here in the manner in which it hides in its shell. Being a "side-necked" turtle, it places its very long neck sideways between carapace and plastron (page 20). It also comes from a different part of the world than the others, namely Australia, which has placed an embargo on its export. But some breeders have succeeded in raising Snake-necked Turtles in sizeable numbers and keeping pet stores supplied. Because of its unusual appearance, the friendly grin on its face, and environmental conditions that are easy to meet, this turtle makes a good pet, although even young ones are quite expensive.

**Size:** 10 to 12 inches (25–30 cm).
**Habitat:** The Snake-necked Turtle is found in eastern Australia where it inhabits ponds and puddles and slow-moving streams. It likes to hide along shallow, muddy banks under the cover of branches and stones. During the rainy season it sometimes lives on land.

**Environmental Needs:** This turtle is used to warm summers and mild winters comparable to the climate of Central Europe, but it is also found in areas where it is warm all year round and the summers are long and wet. In the terrarium it should therefore have air temperatures between 75° and 82°F (24°–28°C) and water temperatures from 73° to 82°F (23°–28°C).

**Behavior:** This turtle likes to swim around actively during the day and needs a fairly large aquarium. It generally gets along well with other turtles, but during the mating season it is aggressive and bites and must be kept singly at least at that time. It also goes after food with great vigor and may bite competitors in the process, so that on the whole I would recommend that you keep this turtle singly at all times.

**Food:** Mixed, with a strong emphasis (80–90%) on water creatures such as snails, crustaceans, and fish.

**Hibernation:** No.

# Terrariums—Size and Equipment

## The Terrarium—Commercial or Home-Made?

Ready-made terrariums are available in different sizes and styles. It pays to invest in good quality and solid workmanship because in all likelihood the terrarium will be your pet's home for many years to come. Commercially available terrariums may be too small for the needs of your turtle (pages 8–9).

The only turtles that may temporarily be housed in a smaller terrarium are the ones that live in water. These turtles can manage in a smaller area because they have a third dimension available to move in, namely, the depth of the water. One or two baby turtles measuring about two inches (4 cm) can be kept initially (up to one or two years, when they will have grown to five or six inches [12–15 cm]) with the following equipment:

A plastic aquarium (holding 8 to 10 gallons [30–40 liters]) with a cover; a thermostatically controlled heater of about 30 watts that maintains a water temperature of about 80°F (26°–27°C); a thermometer measuring the water temperature; a fair-sized piece of cork bark to serve as an island for the turtles to rest on; a desk lamp of 60 watts that swings out on an articulated arm and can be adjusted to shine on the cork island from a distance of about one foot to simulate sunlight. If all this is provided, young water turtles can live in relative comfort in a small terrarium. Young land turtles, on the other hand, need a full-sized terrarium from the beginning because they can move only on a plane.

If you are handy with tools and like to make things, you should build the terrarium yourself according to your own calculations and desires. Of course, you can also have it built to your specifications.

Whether or not you decide to do the work yourself, remember when you choose the materials that wood quickly discolors and eventually rots even in a desert terrarium because the bath has to

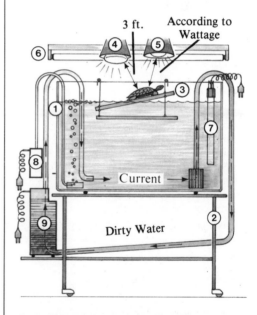

This is the way an aquarium for water turtles should look: Glass container (1) on a movable stand (2) and with an island for sunbathing (3), and ultra-violet lamp (4) for sunshine, a heat lamp (5), and a neon lamp (6) for light. The thermostatically regulated aquarium heater (7) should not be completely submerged. The air pump (8) aerates the water. The circulating pump (9) filters it.

be filled regularly and the plants watered. Plastic pans with sides of plexiglass and screening are better than wood. The construction method of aquariums, i.e., glueing glass panels into aluminum corner pieces, has worked out well for terrariums, too. Plexiglass has the drawback of scratching easily and cracking from prolonged exposure to ultraviolet light.

There is not much room for imagination in setting up the home of a water turtle. You can either choose a plain basin that is easy to keep clean, or you can decorate the turtle's living space with plants. This, of course, requires more money and more elaborate maintenance, and the basin has to be larger since some of the space will be taken up by the land area.

If you are drawn to an all-glass terrarium or aquarium because it looks more elegant than one with a steel or aluminum frame, do not forget that the frame contributes to the strength of the structure and protects the glass edges.

## Useful Technical Accessories

• An ultraviolet lamp of 300 watts to be placed at a distance of about three feet (1 meter) from the terrarium and one of the following:
• A heat lamp, e.g., an infrared lamp of 250 watts, that will heat a dark surface of about 12 × 12 inches (30 cm × 30 cm) from a distance of 20 inches (50 cm) to 122°F (50°C) at the center and 92°F (33°C) at the edges, or a focusing lamp, that will warm a dark surface of 12 × 12 inches (30 cm × 30 cm) from a distance of 4 feet (120 cm) to 95°F (35°C) at the center and 85°F (30°C) at the edges, or a parabolic lamp, that, at a distance of 12 inches, will heat the same size surface to 105°F (44°C) at the center and 82°F (28°C) at the edges.

With any one of these heat lamps, which can be chosen to suit the height of the terrarium, the desired degree of "sunshine" can be produced in a small area.
• A fluorescent tube for general lighting and for plant growth.
• Cables for bottom heating.
• Water heater: The cable leading to the heating element should be installed above water level and perhaps at an angle in such a way that it cannot be chewed through. Surround the heater with roots so that it cannot be knocked over.
• A circulation pump (only for water turtles).
• An aeration pump for the water, which also serves to raise the humidity of the air.
• A stand on rollers that can be locked in place.
• A water thermometer that registers temperatures from about 32° to 100°F (0°–40°C).
• A hygrometer.

# Terrariums — Size and Equipment

## Climate

The climate in the terrarium is regulated by varying the proportion of glass and mesh (with openings of about $\frac{3}{16}$ inches or 4 mm), which lets air pass through. A dry terrarium usually has glass sides and a screen cover, but a water basin has to be at least partially covered if the humidity of the air is to be raised with an aerating pump. By varying the size of the opening in the glass we can adjust humidity at will.

Glass should never be placed between the heat or ultraviolet lamp and the turtle. Not only can the glass crack, but it also interferes with the passage of the light and deprives the animal of its benefits.

## Bottom and Bottom Heat

For land as well as water turtles we cover the bottom of the terrarium with a one-to-one mixture of sand and peat that is free of fertilizers. Combining dry sand with peat that is first soaked and then squeezed as dry as possible produces the proper dampness. Usually a depth of about 4 inches (10 cm) is adequate. Peat discolors the water somewhat, which does not bother the turtles in the least, but if you prefer you can omit the peat and use pure washed sand instead. This kind of bottom packs more solidly than one with peat, and it can get too wet or too dry so that eggs that are buried in it can go undetected and dry out or suffocate.

A heating cable placed in a spiral shape beneath a stone slab should heat the stone to about 97°F (36°C). This can be done with the aid of an electronic thermostat or by choosing a slab of the right thickness so that the temperature at the upper surface will rise to about 97°F, after warming up for several hours, and stay there. Make sure that all the animals in the terrarium have access to the heat sources (light and stone). If this is not the case, the heated surface should be enlarged or supplemented by a second one. If the bottom slab heats up gradually in the course of the morning, stays at about 97°F for a couple of hours in the middle of the day, and then gradually cools down somewhat, this is all right because it parallels the natural temperature fluctuations of the soil. If nobody is at home during the day to turn the heat on and off, a timer should be used.

Warming the soil for land and water turtles: The terrarium floor (1) is insulated with a layer of styrofoam (2) and three layers of aluminum foil (3). The heating cable (4), which warms the stone or cement plate (5), is laid on top of the aluminum.

# *Terrariums — Size and Equipment*

## Decorations

Landscaping a large terrarium is relatively simple and usually produces pleasing results. Arranging a terrarium of minimum proportions is more difficult. It is up to us to balance our sense of beauty with the basic needs of a turtle. We can meet these needs best if we try to look at the world from the point of view of a turtle and put ourselves in the animal's place. This we can do, of course, only if we are familiar with its natural biotope and its need for exercise. The turtle should encounter as many different surfaces and angles as possible as it moves around in the terrarium.

The turtle should be able to walk around or climb over rocks and branches or roots, and there should be corners and caves where it can search for food, rest, and hide.

This terrarium, which is sufficiently large and properly decorated, meets the needs of a land turtle. The rock arrangement increases the amount of usable surface.

# Terrariums — Size and Equipment

If we have a turtle that climbs well, we may, for considerations of weight, want to offer tree limbs rather than rocks. These limbs are placed at a slight angle and must be wide enough for the turtle to walk on them comfortably. If the terrarium has a solid floor, we can build rock terraces. It is advisable to keep the decorations more or less the same for the duration of the turtle's life, so that it can live in a familiar territory where it knows its way around. Of course it is all right to remove a dead plant occasionally or change the bottom material, but if we keep changing around the bath, places for climbing and sunning, and other decorations and equipment, this has an unsettling effect on the animal and keeps it from being relaxed.

## Planting

Plants are not essential to the turtle's well-being, but they help to produce a harmonious effect and appeal to our aesthetic sense.

Water Basin

The floor of the water basin for land turtles should have sloping sides. The water level should never be higher than the forward edge of the carapace (arrow).

Plants must be located where climbing and plant-eating animals cannot get at them. Otherwise they will not last long. Only relatively undemanding plants that do well in the climate that prevails in the terrarium should be chosen. You can consult specialized literature or ask for advice at the nursery where you are buying the plants. Quite apart from their aesthetic appeal, healthy plants that fit in with the terrarium's biotope help maintain a constant climate which we should check if the plants begin to look unhealthy.

## The Water Basin

A *land turtle* needs a place with water as much as it needs air. It may move across the dry sand covered with dust most of the time, but it still needs access to cool water. In the wild, the turtle has plenty of opportunities to avoid dehydration. Humidity in the soil, dew, rain, fresh food, or resorting to "dry sleep" (page 16) keep this armored expert in survival from dying of thirst. We have no way of regulating the turtle's absorption of moisture through the stomach and the skin by supplying dew, rain, or ground water and therefore have to offer an appropriate drinking and bathing basin that is always full of clean water of the same temperature as the bottom of the terrarium. A gentle slope in the water basin will encourage the animal to linger when it drinks or bathes without having to raise its head above water in a tiring position. In contrast to the overall size

# Terrariums — Size and Equipment

of the terrarium, the water basin for a baby turtle should not be as large as for a grown animal. Such a basin would be too deep and the baby turtle could drown in it. The size of the bath is increased as the turtle grows. This can be done by placing a shallow bowl (e.g., the saucer of a flower pot) inside the adult-sized bath that is then filled up to the saucer's rim with sand. When the turtle is large enough, saucer and sand can be removed and the original basin filled with water.

For *water turtles* the water in the built-in basin must always be deeper than the turtle's shell is wide. Otherwise, if the animal falls, it could end up in the water on its back. Unable to right itself, it will drown.

The surface of the basin should be rough for both water and land turtles so that they can get a good hold with their claws and are in no danger of slipping.

## Outdoor Terrariums

If your turtle comes from a temperate zone (i.e., Europe, the Near East, or North America) it can be housed outdoors during the warm weather. A safely enclosed run or a small pond in the garden or any draft-free place (be careful if you have a windy balcony!) with sunlight strong enough to heat up the terrarium to around 85°F (30°C) for at least two or three hours will do (be sure to check the temperature!).

Turtles from tropical regions can be kept outdoors only in exceptionally warm weather with constantly high temperatures. If you can move the terrarium with the animal in it, you can place it in a sunny spot where the rays of the sun can reach the turtle without passing through glass. If you do this, the turtle always has to have a shady spot to retire to, or it may die of heat stroke. If

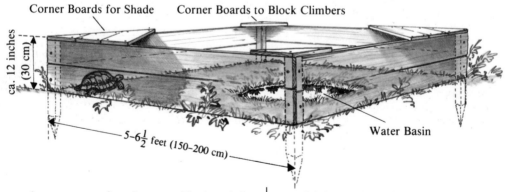

An escape-proof outdoor run. The boards in the enclosure should be strong and the corner posts sunk deep into the ground. It is essential that you provide shade and block routes the turtle could use to climb out.

36

# Terrariums — Size and Equipment

You can prevent your land turtle from escaping from your yard by placing a close-mesh fence deep into the ground or by mounting it on a wall that sets into the ground.

you have an escape-proof garden (surrounded by walls or fine-meshed wire that is dug into the ground), the turtle can run free as long as there are no steep pits or walls that could cause an accident. A fence made of boards and corner posts will keep the turtle from wandering too far without depriving it of enjoying natural sunlight and grass. **Caution:** Turtles like to dig and can work their way under fences!

## The Quarantine Terrarium

In order to take the hygienic precautions that are necessary for the care of turtles (page 52) we have to have another container, a quarantine terrarium that dispenses with all decorations and is designed to meet only the most basic needs of the turtle. A plain glass aquarium that offers a darkened corner for hiding in and is kept absolutely clean works best for this purpose. This quarantine terrarium is used for treating diseases. This way other turtles are protected from contamination, and the sick animal is less likely to reinfect itself from its own excrement.

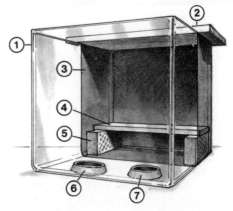

A quarantine terrarium for land turtles. A quarantine terrarium cannot be decorated. Glass aquarium (1) 24 × 21 × 21 inches (60 × 50 × 50 cm) with a board cover (2) and adhesive foil (3) on the outside to provide a darker area. A board (4) and bricks (5) form a cave. Food and water bowls (6, 7) are on the terrarium floor.

# Basic Rules for Care

## Proper Acclimation

If we do not know how the turtle we have acquired has been kept we should not place it right away in a terrarium we have prepared and outfitted beforehand. Instead we bathe the newcomer first in a bowl of lukewarm water (82°F [28°C]) to which we have added one tablespoon of salt per quart of water. If you buy your* turtle from a dealer there is no way of telling if the animal is suffering from dehydration or some other disease. A lukewarm bath softens dried-on dirt and fecal matter, allows the animal to quench its thirst, and, with the addition of salt, counteracts possible previous loss of salts due to diarrhea. When the animal is ready to leave the water, we clean it, check shell and skin for injuries, and examine folds in the skin for mites and ticks as well as other signs of illness (page 51). If the turtle looks healthy and lively, it is placed in the terrarium. It can then search out a hiding place where it is allowed to remain until it chooses of its own free will to come out again. We can, of course, entice it by offering fresh food every day. Usually a plant eater will start eating after one or two days, a meat or fish eater anywhere between one and five days. The turtle will behave differently if it has some internal disorder that cannot be detected from the outside (take it to the veterinarian!), if it was rudely roused from hibernating, or if it is in a quiescent state similar to hibernation. You can see that there is good reason not to buy a turtle from a temperate zone during its hibernating season (October to April). It is generally a good idea to take a sample of the first stool and have a veterinarian examine it for endoparasites and prescribe treatment, if needed (page 48). Old pill bottles with a drop of water to keep the stool moist serve well as containers. If you cannot get to the veterinarian right away, the sample can be kept in the refrigerator up to a week this way.

**Please observe:** After you place the turtle in the terrarium, watch it to see which corner it sleeps in and where it likes to dig and deposit feces and urine (a whitish-yellow, slimy or grainy mass). These "comfort stations" are as essential to the turtle as your favorite armchair is to you after work.

If the turtle defecates outside the water, you should remove the feces together with some of the surrounding soil. Some traces of them may be left. They function as markers, making the territory feel familiar and often causing turtles to use the same spot consistently for defecating. This, of course, helps keep the terrarium clean. Choose a cool, dry spot nearby (not under the lamp) for the feeding place, and place a clean, flat dish (e.g., a saucer of a flower pot) with fresh food there every day.

## Getting Used to Other Animals

Dogs, cats, guinea pigs, and mice must not be allowed to get near the newly acquired turtle, because their curiosity,

# Basic Rules for Care

playfulness, or instinct for gnawing can be fatal, particularly to a young turtle. If the newcomer is to be housed together with other turtles, we must make sure there is ample room for "comfort stations" for everyone and that all the individuals belong to species that get along peaceably with each other. Proceed with caution in the case of water turtles (page 21 ff). If you notice that the old-timers are defending their territory and pushing the new animal off into a corner, you will have to remove them for a few days or weeks to the quarantine terrarium (page 37) and then experiment with returning them to their regular home. Wait until the newcomer finds his way around easily in his new environment and the old-timers have lost some of their cocky self-assurance from having been deprived of their usual quarters. Then they, too, will have to go through some readjustment, and nobody will have a headstart on anyone else.

This phase of adjustment is a strain for all the animals but especially for the new one, and if additional outside disturbances or changes in the environment (technical defects, unreliable vacation care, etc.) compound the situation, it may become critical for the animals' health. Watch them with special care at such times so that any weakness or incipient illness can be spotted and treated instantly. The basic rule is, as always, to avoid anything that could cause stress. To enumerate such causes would take up more space than we have in this little book and is superfluous if the rules for optimal care provided here are followed.

## Everyday Life With Your Turtle

You now have enough information to establish your turtle's everyday living conditions and provide it with variety and change. In nature the animal is exposed to many external stimuli and challenges. It has to cope with heat and cold, wind and rain, and it has to conquer steep slopes and deep crevasses. Terrestrial turtles are good at climbing and like to do it. If your turtle seems too phlegmatic, lure it up and down rocks and roots across the terrarium before you let it chomp on a favorite tidbit of food. Simulate rain with lukewarm water from a spray bottle, make the sun shine, leave the land area unheated (i.e., at room temperature) for a day, change your turtle's diet with the seasons from fresh and juicy foods to drier ones, like hay. Your turtle will respond to such changes with greater vitality.

## Trips, Long and Short

If we have to break the turtle's routine and move it, there are some important points we have to consider for the sake of the animal's health.
**Short Trips:** A trip home or to the veterinarian, let alone being shipped by mail, represents a trauma for the turtle that can make it ill. There are two main dangers: lack of air and hypothermia. The first of these dangers is minor in the case of short trips. Because of their slow metabolism, turtles do not need as much oxygen as mammals do, for instance. A

# Basic Rules for Care

full-grown turtle of any of the species listed in this book can therefore travel, without any ill effects, for five to six hours in a special air-tight plastic terrarium of about 8 gallons (30 liters) capacity. This fact is neither a justification for "experiments in survival" nor an excuse for closing the travel terrarium with an air-tight cover in the summer, but knowing about the turtle's minimal air requirements is useful in wintertime.

Transporting a turtle in outside temperatures below 65° to 70°F (18°–20°C) can have disastrous results. Since a well-aired terrarium always makes cool air available to the animal, we should cover a travel terrarium with a tightly fitting cover (tape air slits shut). Do not leave the turtle shut up like this for more than five or six hours. Then remove the cover in a warm room and fan fresh air into the terrarium. Ordinarily this is not necessary because the trip to your veterinarian is unlikely to take so long.

The supply of warm air for breathing is thus taken care of. What about heat? Line the carrier in which you place the terrarium with several layers of newspaper to insulate the terrarium from the outside cold. Then place a hot-water bottle filled with water at 115°F (45°C) or a Kool-Pac (ice substitute used in picnic coolers) heated to this temperature underneath the terrarium, and cover the top with another layer of several newspapers.

**Caution:** Turtles used to a tropical climate can catch cold during even brief exposures to temperatures of 60°F (15°C) or below. The cold can easily turn into pneumonia or some other illness, since terrarium turtles are generally somewhat spoiled and have less resistance. In addition to providing heat and air we have to see to it that the turtle does not slip around helplessly on the plastic bottom of the travel terrarium. A layer of dry foam rubber provides a good grip for the turtle's claws. Now you are ready to transport your water or land turtle safely. Never take your water turtle anywhere in a container full of water, where it would bob around helplessly. Nor is it advisable to moisten the foam rubber, because evaporating water creates cold which is just as harmful to the animal as cold air. Depending on the species, a turtle can also be transported with less elaborate preparations in a dry linen bag that must be securely tied at the top. Make sure the seam is on the outside. It has happened more than once that a turtle caught its claws in the threads of the seam, got entangled and strangled itself. The requirements for air and warmth are just the same as for a trip in a travel terrarium.

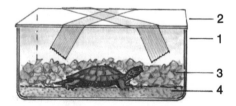

For transporting water turtles short distances, you can use a plastic terrarium (1) with a closely fitting cover (2). The floor should be covered with foam rubber, both cubes (3) and a mat (4).

# Basic Rules for Care

**Longer Trips:** Unfortunately it is not advisable to take turtles along on trips to the sunny south. Not only is long-term confinement to a car, where it is usually either too hot or too drafty, harmful; but it is also very likely that the turtle will refuse to eat on the trip. It goes on a hunger strike because it is torn out of its familiar surroundings and territory and forced to undergo changes in its environment. The resulting stress may well bring on general weakness and disease that end in death.

## Vacation Care

You can leave your turtle unattended for a day without worry if the terrarium is constructed in an "accident-proof" manner as described on pages 31–37; and, in the case of a land turtle, if there is no chance of its drowning. A day of fasting does no harm if the turtle is healthy; in fact many experienced keepers of reptiles prescribe periodic fasting. A beginner should not be in a hurry to follow this advice, however. He should wait until he gets the "feel" of what is good for his turtle. A day of fasting is worthy of mention only for plant-eating turtles which depend on getting fresh food daily. Turtles that prefer meat or fish are fed less frequently in any case (page 45).

Illnesses occur with greater frequency when you are away on vacation. Anyone who deals with pets knows that. The explanation is obvious. Many stand-in caretakers are either unable or unwilling to pay as much attention to the pet as you do. Not everyone has a gift for looking after animals, and only careful observation and attention can prevent upsets in digestion and behavior. Possibilities for contact with other terrarium buffs who might be willing to substitute for you are mentioned on page 73. Friends and neighbors are usually complete neophytes without any previous experience for their task, and pet boarding houses are often booked up or overcrowded. As a consequence of all this feedings are often irregular and one-sided during vacation, heating and aeration are not properly adjusted, and hygiene is neglected. All these aspects of care are, as we know by now, essential to the health of our pets.

Since hardly anybody is willing to forego his vacation on account of a turtle, we are faced with the question: How do we forestall possible disaster? Explain to your neighbor in detail what the normal behavior and the special idiosyncrasies of your turtle are (e.g., it likes to spend half the day in the water). Draw his or her attention to possible changes of behavior by pointing out applicable sections in this book (especially the special chapter "Understanding Turtles," pages 60ff.), and leave the name and address of a veterinarian who knows about turtles. Show the caretaker how much food the turtle gets per day or per week and go over the menu plan you are following at the time (write down the kinds of fruit, the vitamin supplements, in short, all the necessary foods).

# Basic Rules for Care

If you are unable to find a willing neighbor, you may have no choice but to board your turtle. Often the best bet is an experienced private keeper of reptiles whose animals you can look after in exchange later (page 73). Such a boarding home is a relatively good solution even if you have to send your turtle there by mail.

Pet stores and professional boarding homes for pets are sometimes willling to take care of turtles for a daily fee. If you decide to take this course, be sure to inspect the place yourself beforehand.

## Wintering Over Indoors

In October, when the light intensity lessens and the days get shorter, our turtle, if it is a native of temperate climes, will become less active. When it stops eating for several days in a row that is a signal that we should stop feeding it. Instead the turtle should be bathed daily for at least ten minutes in warm water (75° to 80°F [24°-26°C]) to encourage complete voiding of the intestine. (Even before this, in the first part of September, the turtle should be thoroughly checked for internal parasites and be given worm medicine if necessary.) Now the feces should be examined once more for worms and for the state of nutrition (page 48) to make sure the turtle is ready for hibernation. After these preparations, water turtles from temperate zones can be left at the bottom of the terrarium without food and in clean cool water (40°-47°F [4°-8°C]) that has been allowed to cool down over a period of two to three weeks. There they will rest for one to two months. Getting a land turtle set up for hibernation is more complex.

After bathing the turtle we turn the heater off and let the temperature in the terrarium drop to about 68°F (20°C). If the turtle's activity slows down as a result of this, it is time to move the

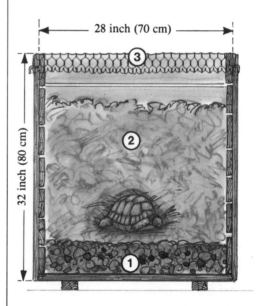

For wintering your turtle over in your cellar, use a roomy wooden box in which you place a layer of clay beads (1). Next comes a layer of leaves, wood shavings, or peat moss (2). Then the box should be covered with screening or close-mesh chicken wire (3).

# Basic Rules for Care

animal to its winter quarters where the temperature should range between 42° and 45°F (5°–7°C). A cellar is the best place for the winter quarters. For a grown turtle you should prepare a box no smaller than 28 × 28 × 28 to 32 inches (70 cm × 70 cm × 70–80 cm) with cracks $\frac{1}{16}$ to $\frac{1}{8}$ inch (2 mm) wide between the boards so that enough air can enter through the sides.

The bottom of the box is covered with 4 inches (10 cm) of dampened — not wet — lava clinker or fired clay beads (both available at gardening supply stores) to serve as a moisture reservoir. Then fill the box to about three fourths full with almost dry but not stiff peat moss (also available at gardening supply stores).

Instead of peat moss you can use clean, almost dry but not brittle oak or beech leaves or wood chips from resinous trees or from oaks or beeches. Your aim, which is not altogether easy to achieve, is to create an environment that is fairly dry but still damp enough to prevent desiccation of the turtle's body.

A wire-screen cover will keep the turtle from falling out of its box should it walk in its sleep, and it also prevents mice and rats from nibbling at the motionless and defenseless animal.

Check every two weeks to make sure the turtle is hibernating safely.

If you winter over several animals, the box must be larger and subdivided so that one turtle's sleep is not disturbed by the restless digging of another which, for one reason or another, cannot settle down properly or wakes up too early.

## Wintering Over Outdoors

Wintering over a turtle outside is much simpler. Watch where the turtle digs itself in (often underneath some bushes), protect the spot against rats by placing a piece of fine wire screen about six by six feet (150 cm × 150 cm) over it and pile about 18 inches (45 cm) of leaves or straw over that. This will keep the turtle from freezing.

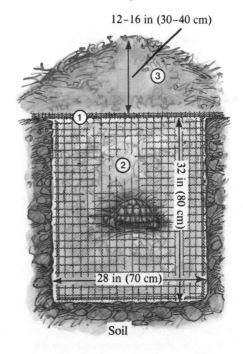

12–16 in (30–40 cm)

③

①

②

32 in (80 cm)

28 in (70 cm)

Soil

Your turtle can winter outdoors in a wire cage sunk into the ground (1). The cage is then filled with leaves, wood shavings, or peat moss (2) and covered with straw or leaves (3).

Or you can dig a pit of the same dimensions suggested above for a box, line the walls with fine wire mesh (against rodents), and fill the hole with dry leaves. When the turtle is settled in the leaves, you fasten a wire screen cover to the sides, thus creating a tight-fitting basket, which you then cover with about one foot (30 cm) of straw or leaves. This method has the advantage that the moisture in the soil keeps the turtle from drying out.

**Premature or Seasonal Waking**

If the temperature in the cellar rises considerably above the ideal of 42° to 45°F (5°–7°C) because the winter is unseasonably warm or because spring is coming, the turtle will wake up and must be returned to the terrarium when you next check on it. You resume normal care while the temperature gradually rises in the course of three or four days to the usual terrarium conditions. *It is crucial to give the turtle a leisurely bath before any feeding so that it can absorb enough water to make up for the loss of fluid during hibernation. Only then may you offer it food.*

**First Feeding After Hibernation**

Not all turtles are ready to eat as soon as they wake up. Some first have to get their bearings again. This can take two to five days or, in some cases, as long as two to two-and-a-half weeks. During this period the metabolic rate is adjusted from hibernation to normal activity.

In order to tell whether a post-hibernation lack of appetite is normal or a sign of illness we can test the turtle's vitality (page 51). If the animal seems to be in a weakened state a visit to the veterinarian may be advisable. If not, you can let another week pass without worry.

**When Should You Not Induce Hibernation?**

Very young and therefore small turtles should receive normal care in "summery" temperatures year round because they usually do not have enough food reserves to survive a lengthy pause in feeding.

Once a turtle is two to three years old, or considerably older, this would apply only if it is undernourished (page 47), if it is infested with endoparasites, or if it is ill with a cold, for instance (page 49).

Turtles that do not hibernate for one reason or another or that wake up early can be kept in the terrarium under summer conditions without problems.

In my experience even turtles that were active continually for several years in a row without any hibernating breaks suffered no ill effects except that their sexual activity was arrested. Judging from the many cases in which this happened, it seems that loss of fertility is often the price paid for omitting hibernation.

# Diet and Feeding

## Importance of a Varied Diet

It is not easy to provide a turtle with the varied diet Mother Nature offers it. But we should at least make an effort and make full use of our inventiveness.

In its natural habitat the turtle finds grasses, bushes and other plants that flower and bear fruits. We, too, should entice the turtle's appetite with all kinds of plants (unless it is a pure meat-eater) from kitchen herbs to hay. Blossoms, fruits, and seeds from wildflowers are suitable foods for turtles as are wild and cultivated berries, fruit, lettuce, any member of the cabbage family, and many other plants. Make sure, though, not to offer poisonous plants.

Any food must be chopped to bite size so that it can be swallowed in two or three gulps. If a turtle starts to favor one particular food, we omit that delicacy from the daily fare for a while and force the animal to eat the less palatable but often healthier foods such as bulky, fibrous stems. In this way we keep the turtle from getting an unbalanced diet, the digestive system stays healthy, and the animal does not overeat.

If the turtle eats animal proteins as well as plants, we offer it anything in the line of insects, snails (with and without shells), worms, and beetles it might find in nature, all freshly killed. On the whole this menu appeals to both water and land turtles. Water turtles also enjoy eating insect larvae.

Pure meat-eaters—and this includes many water turtles—can, in addition to

This turtle has been overfed. Because of excessive fat, it can no longer fully retract its arms and legs inside its shell.

the above, be given small fish (cut up gold fish and bait fish), thin strips of lean beef heart (pork is too fatty), and sliced filets of larger fresh-water fish. Purely vegetarian and omnivorous turtles are fed five to six times a week, preferably twice on the same day and during their main period of activity. Leftovers, particularly if they have fallen in the water, are removed when the turtle is resting.

Pure carnivores are fed about twice a week since their digestion works more slowly and the food lasts longer. Scraps from preparing our own food can be a cheap source of fresh greens and raw meat and add to the nutritive value of a turtle's diet.

45

# Diet and Feeding

## Supplements: Vitamins, Calcium, Trace Elements

Dried cat food is a good supplement because it is enriched with vitamins and trace elements. By including a little cat food we save ourselves the trouble of adding vitamins, which we would have to do otherwise in the following quantities: one drop each of vitamins A, D, and E (available at pet stores and drug stores) and one drop of a multivitamin that includes the B-complex vitamins three times a week. The turtle should also get a bit of mixed calcium and trace minerals (available at pet stores and drug stores) twice a week. This powder can be mixed into a small ball of lean hamburger or stirred into moistened dry feed.

## A Special Dish

In conclusion, I am going to share with you a "secret recipe" from the kitchen of a successful turtle breeder. This recipe will enable you to create a meal that will not only appeal to your turtle, no matter what its tastes, but also contains all the necessary nutrients and supplements. Although this miracle dish is meant as nothing more than the turtle's "meat and potatoes"—comparable to an improved version of dry cat food—it can easily serve as an exclusive diet during vacations and thus considerably simplify food preparation for the caretaker. The recipe is for a "jello salad" that will feed a turtle for a month and can be frozen in daily portions (adjust the amounts to the needs of your turtles).

The ingredients are as follows:

For predominantly vegetarian turtles: 75% to 85% vegetable matter composed of as many different kinds and textures as possible. For meat-eaters: 60% to 70% meat and fish of all kinds, including frozen shrimp and octopus, raw liver, and eggs; in short, any animal protein except fats and pork.

The rest of the 100 percent (measured in weight) is made up of foods of the opposite class, i.e., herbivores get 80% plant material and 20% animal proteins, and carnivores get the larger percentage in meat and fish.

After all the ingredients are washed, they are ground up in an electric mixer and should produce a liquid with the consistency of honey. Heat this mixture to about 175°F (80°C), stirring constantly to keep it from burning and from coming to a boil, which would destroy nutrients. Let it cool to about 140°F (60°C) and mix in gelatin powder along with one teaspoon of mixed minerals (e.g., Osspulvit, made by Madaus) and one quarter of a vitamin pill (e.g., Supradin, made by Roche) per quart. Dissolve the vitamin pill in a little water before adding it, and use somewhat more gelatin than the directions call for because the jello may otherwise dissolve in the warm water of the terrarium. It is very important to stir the mixture thoroughly before it starts to jell so that the supplements are evenly distributed.

# Diet and Feeding

When the mass has jelled, cut it into individual servings and freeze in plastic bags. Later you can take out one package at a time, thaw it, cut it into strips, and feed these to the turtle. You create the flavor that appeals to your turtle by adding an extra handful of your turtle's favorite fruit, vegetable, or meat. One side benefit of this method of feeding is that there are hardly any leftovers to soil the water. As I have already said, this miracle food by itself is no substitute for fresh foods and should consequently not be used as a steady diet over long periods of time without the addition of fresh tidbits. But it is very handy during periods when we cannot devote as much attention to the care of our turtle as usual.

## Watch Out when Feeding Water Turtles

If two animals of different sizes are kept together, the larger one can easily bite off the smaller one's head if both go after the same morsel at the same time. As a general rule, land turtles should get their food served on a shallow dish on land, and water turtles should be fed in the water.

## Amounts of Food

There is no prescribed amount of food for turtles. Like other wild animals, turtles living in nature take advantage of the seasons when food is abundant to stuff themselves in anticipation of the lean times ahead. If we do not impose lean times of our own making, the turtle will go on stuffing itself until it literally runs out of room in its shell and is unable to pull in its arms and legs all the way because of the rolls of fat (drawing, page 45).

Use the following rule as a guideline: The thighs of a properly nourished turtle are round and feel solid to the touch; in an undernourished animal you can feel the bones through the muscles.

47

# If Your Turtle Gets Sick

Since you are by now taking excellent care of your turtle you should not have to deal with illnesses at all. But just in case, I am going to describe the most common ailments that beset a turtle and how to treat them.

(If your veterinarian has not had much experience with turtles, show him this chapter. The information in it is based primarily on cases treated at the Exotarium of the Frankfurt Zoo and has thus been tested in practice.)

## Disorders of the Digestive System

**Salmonella:** Their presence in the intestine is normal and has to be treated only in cases of serious intestinal disorders (prolonged diarrhea, anorexia).

Mix 50 mg chloramphenicol per 2 lb (1 kg) of body weight in with the food for at least six days or longer as needed until the symptoms disappear. The same treatment applies to the pathogens *Aeromonas* and *Pseudomonas.* They should be treated even if their presence is not clinically established.

**Amoebas:** These should always be treated. Give 62.5 mg of metronidazol, e.g., CLONT (made by Bayer) per 2 lb (1 kg) of body weight. Stop for two weeks, then repeat. (This treatment is suggested in a leaflet of the parasitology department of the University of Hohenheim.)

**Tapeworm:** One dose of 25 mg of praziquantel, e.g., DRONCIT (made by Bayer) per 2 lb (1 kg) of body weight.

**Pinworms:** (Oxyuridae, etc.): Give 50 mg of fenbendazol (= Hoechst's PANACUR) per 2 lb (1 kg) of body weight for five consecutive days and repeat after twenty-one days (for Ascaridae) or fifty-six days (for Oxyuridae).

A veterinarian can diagnose the presence of these pathogens by analyzing a stool sample. He can then prescribe treatment.

**Prolapsed Intestine:** The intestine sticks out of the cloaca and is dragged along the ground. This condition will lead to infection and death if it is not corrected surgically. A prolapsed intestine should not be confused with the swelling of the penis or the anal bladder—a stretching of the wall of the cloaca found in many water turtles—which will recede by itself after a while.

**Constipation:** This can be the result of too much dry food (pellets, hay) together with too dry an environment, insufficient warmth, and lack of exercise.

A bath twice a day for ten minutes in lukewarm water (80°–82°F [27°–28°C]) everyday, until the problem stops, is usually effective.

## Respiratory Infections and Related Disorders

**Pneumonia:** Suspicious symptoms are bubbles or foam at the mouth and/or noisy breathing.

Requires diagnosis by a veterinarian and treatment with proper amounts of antibiotics for the weight of the turtle, just as with mammals.

# If Your Turtle Gets Sick

Remedy the condition that has caused the illness, e.g., temperature too low, drafts, air too dry.

**Swollen Eyelids:** Treat with an antibiotic eye ointment (if there is no fungus infection). Squeeze the ointment between the eye and the lid; it will do no good on the outside of the lid. Remedy possible causes: cold temperatures; drafty location; in the case of water turtles, dirty water.

Swollen eyelids are a sign of grossly inadequate care. They are caused by exposure to drafts and cold or, in water turtles, by dirty or excessively cold water.

## Injuries and Disorders Affecting Shell and Skin

**Softening and Distortion of the Shell:** May be associated with rickets. Treat with natural sunlight in the summer or increase ultraviolet lighting (one-half hour per day from a distance of 3 feet [1 m]); also, one drop of a multivitamin high in vitamin D; sepia or calcium supplements. One to 3 drops of liquid calcium (e.g., Frubiase, made by Dieckmann), depending on the size of the animal, has been found very effective but is very expensive.

Possible causes: Too little natural sunlight, one-sided diet poor in vitamins and minerals.

Fractures of bones and of the shell may cause malformations which will not adversely affect the vitality of the animal once the fracture is healed.

**Peeling of Skin and of Thin Layers of Shell:** It is normal for reptiles to slough off their skin periodically, and the skin of turtles comes off in little bits almost constantly. With water turtles you can occasionally observe a very thin layer of the carapace or the plastron coming off, particularly if they are covered with algae growth. This is still normal, but if there is a repeated shedding of skin or of thick pieces of shell from the same spot, something is wrong. Check for inflammation or fungal infection.

**Wounded Shells—Fractures:** Wounds in a turtle's shell usually heal well. Even a hole in the carapace of a *Testudo pardalis* that exposed part of the spine healed without complications under veterinary care and the administration of an antibiotic powder. Consequently, a turtle whose shell has been broken through a fall or some other injury has a good chance to recover if given proper care. Ordinarily there is no need for a splint because the shell itself is rigid enough.

49

# *If Your Turtle Gets Sick*

**Bites and Skin Conditions:** These can be treated with camomile tea, ointments, or an antibiotic ointment prescribed by a veterinarian.

### General Listlessness and Lack of Appetite

If these symptoms occur outside the hibernating season (October to April), they may signal the initial stages of almost any of the disorders mentioned above and should be read as a warning to watch your turtle with special care.

### Ticks and Mites

Ticks are visible as flat or roundish and usually blackish-brown bodies the size of the head of a pin and solidly

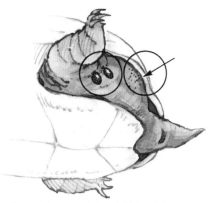

If you discover ticks, which will swell up with the blood they suck (left), or tiny red mites, your turtle requires immediate treatment against them.

lodged on the skin. Mites are small, usually red, moving dots as big as the point of a needle.

Spray the animal and the cage with a .2% solution of Trichlorphon, e.g., NEGUVON (made by Bayer). Repeat eight to ten days later if any remaining eggs have hatched.

### Other Tasks of Routine Care

**Trimming Claws:** Claws that grow too long are not so much a disorder as a sign of poor care. Males of the *Graptemys* and *Chrysemys* genera are an exception.

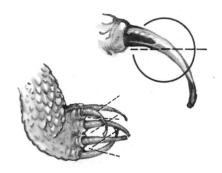

Overly long claws have to be cut back, but be careful that you do not cut into the blood vessels.

The claws on their forefeet naturally grow long and should not be cut. Otherwise all claws that grow too long must be trimmed. They grow too long if the animal does not have a chance to run around on the ground and keep them worn down.

# If Your Turtle Gets Sick

**Trimming the Beak:** If the horny edges of the beak grow too long they have to be filed down. This overgrowth is the result of a diet that is too soft. If harder foods, such as small seeds, cuttlebone, and fibrous vegetable stems are offered, the beak is kept worn down naturally.

**Shell Care:** If land turtles are kept in a somewhat too dry atmosphere, their shells may develop cracks and look unattractive. Rubbing a tiny bit of vaseline into the shell every two or three months keeps the uppermost layers of the shell elastic and improves the turtle's looks without doing any harm.

If the beak grows too long, it has to be filed back. Overgrowth will occur if your turtle is fed only soft foods.

## Health Check

If you wish to check the general health of your turtle — even if there are no obvious signs of illness — it helps if you know what to look for and how to go about it.

• Is the shell solid? Except for very young turtles whose shell is still soft, the shell should be hard and not yield to pressure. (This does not apply to soft-shelled turtles, including the African *Trionyx triunguis*.)

• External parasites: Look especially in the deep folds of the arms and legs (Treatment, see page 50).

• Is the skin free of wounds, bites, sores, and white to reddish inflamed spots (i.e., wounds that are not healing properly)? If not, have the vet diagnose and treat the cause.

• Are the eyes open and clear and without swollen lids or mucous discharge?

• Are the nostrils and mouth free of phlegm and foamy bubbles?

• Is the breathing quiet?

• Is the turtle (land or water) walking with the bottom of its shell parallel to the ground (healthy) or with one side or the hind end dragging along (abnormal)?

• Is the water turtle swimming straight in an almost horizontal position with the rear end lowered just slightly (healthy) or is it at a permanent backward or sideways tilt (abnormal)?

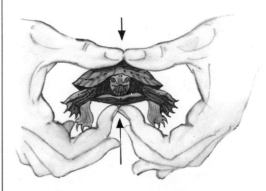

You can test the firmness of the shell by pressing on the back and belly. Be particularly careful when you do this with young turtles.

51

A sick turtle will walk with its shell tilted down in back. A healthy one carries its shell level.

• Is the animal strong enough to hold itself up, using its front feet to hang suspended between your fingers (drawing, page 6)? Turtles that are weakened by hunger or illness will let go and drop to the floor. A healthy turtle will also struggle energetically and persistently to get back on its feet if for some reason it finds itself lying on its back.
• There is no such thing as a "dwarf" or "slow-growing" turtle! Slow or arrested growth is the result of inadequate feeding and care.

### Turtles as Disease Carriers

There are many parasites (amoebas) that live only on turtles and on heterothermous animals in general but that cannot survive at the constant temperature of 98.6°F (37°C) maintained by the human body. That is why the danger of catching these from a turtle is slight.

Many turtles carry an intestinal bacteria called *Salmonella* which is *not* host-specific and can attack humans causing dysentery. Children may have especially low resistance to some species of

*Salmonella* and thus, many states have enacted regulations relating to health and the sale of turtles. The New York State Department of Health, for example, has a regulation Number 2.58 in the state sanitary code which provides that after October 29, 1974, turtles sold in the state of New York must be free of *Salmonella* or other infection-causing bacterial organisms.

### Terrarium Hygiene

**Land Turtles:** Even if you remove feces and urine, flaked-off skin, and leftover food regularly, fine dirt will gradually accumulate in the sand and become a breeding ground for germs. The area near the water basin where it is warm and damp provides ideal conditions for pathogens and worm eggs or larvae to thrive and keep reinfecting your turtle. It is therefore extremely important not to let things get that far and to replace the bottom material at regular intervals, say,

If a water turtle swims tilted to one side, it is ill. In such cases, it is often the lungs and/or anal bladder that are affected.

◁ Birth of a long-necked turtle, *Chelodina oblonga*. Above: Hatching out of the egg and the embryo.
Below: This newly hatched baby turtle is able to live on its own and requires no care from its parents.

every three to six months, depending on the cleanliness of the animal and whether or not it has worms. If your particular turtle is free of worms, keeps pretty clean, and defecates in only a few places that are easy to clean, replacing the sand twice a year will be sufficient. If, however, the excreta are all over the terrarium and smeared into the sand, the chore has to be done every three months. But regardless of your animal's habits, if an amoeba or *Pseudomonas* or worm infection has been detected and is being treated, the bottom material has to be changed and the terrarium or swimming basin sprayed with a 3% formalin solution (make seams airtight, spray, and keep covered for twenty-four hours).

Since formalin has a strong and unpleasant smell and a turtle's olfactory organs are very sensitive (page 61), it would be sheer torture for the animal if you put it back into the terrarium before the smell is completely gone. To determine the right time we should not rely on our own sense of smell, which is rather underdeveloped by turtle standards, but let the animal be the judge. Mere traces of the disinfectant will appear to it as an overpowering stench. We should therefore wait at least a week after we think the smell is completely gone before returning the turtle to the terrarium. This is, of course, assuming that the animal is completely cured of the parasites. One way to render the formalin completely harmless is to spray with a 30% hydrogen peroxide solution that converts the formalin into formic acid which can then be washed off with water.

**Water Turtles:** The general rules for land turtles also apply to water turtles. We proceed basically just as for land turtles, but because turtles living in the water also have healthy appetites and void in the water and because food leftovers decompose rapidly in warm water, it is necessary to change the entire contents of the basin once a day. (Depending on the size of the turtle and of the basin this may have to be done only every two or three days.) If you neglect this chore, the bacteria in the water may multiply to the point where they cause illness. It is easy to recognize such a dangerous situation by the visible "bacterial" clouding of the water. Running a filter is no substitute for changing the water! Most of the food and excreta are indeed removed from the basin, but they stay in the filter chamber where they decay and pollute the water with harmful decomposition agents and products. We should therefore not only change the water but also remove any excreta before feeding and clean up leftover food afterwards. Only if there are about twenty-five gallons of water per pound of turtle can you get away with changing the water only once or twice a week.

# Breeding Turtles

Having enough space for parents as well as offspring is the first prerequisite for breeding turtles. (One hatching will produce five to eight turtle babies which should grow up in a separate terrarium.) Another necessary condition is that the prospective parents have reached sexual maturity. In European land turtles this is the case when they are three to five years old. European marsh turtles do not mature sexually until they reach the age of ten to twelve years. Most other species range somewhere in between. If we have a male and a female of the appropriate age, we can simply house them together and let nature take its course. Healthy, non-aggressive turtles will mate sooner or later, and in time the female will deposit her eggs.

## Planned Breeding

We can encourage reproduction by stimulating the readiness to copulate. This is done by separating the partners for a month or two before the planned time of mating. We simply move the male or the female into the terrarium that is later going to house the offspring. For most tropical and subtropical turtles, mating time, which is determined by a number of external stimuli, such as the length of day, occurs in the spring, usually somewhere between the end of April and the end of May. Since hibernating turtles usually do not wake up until about this time, no additional segregation during the waking state is necessary.

Rising temperatures play an important part in inducing readiness to mate. Turtles that do not rest in the winter should therefore spend their time away from the mate in temperatures that lie about 10°F (4°–5°C) below the maximum for both air and water, and the period of sunlight should be cut down from the normal eight to twelve hours to approximately six hours per day. After this regimen—or after hibernation—the pair is brought together, and the temperature is raised over a period of three to four weeks to a "summery" peak. At the same time we increase the "length of day" to about twelve hours and imitate spring showers by spraying the ground with water and keeping it a little moister than usual.

Land turtles mating. The male makes the female stand still by ramming her. Then he climbs onto her back.

# Breeding Turtles

In addition we offer delicate and juicy greens or fresh meat to eat. The animals are bound to respond to this springtime abundance and proceed first to engage in courtship display and then to mating.

Describing these events makes them sound easier than they often are in reality. Incompatibility of the partners, physical immaturity, previous illnesses, or confinement in too small a terrarium are all obstacles to reproduction. Soft-shelled turtles (Trionychidae) often behave aggressively toward each other. The Cologne Zoo has built a special breeding section in its aquarium to allow turtles to get away from each other and meet only for mating. This way even unsociable animals can be brought together without ill consequences. The set-up at the Cologne Zoo consists of an aquarium with a glass divider. The two partners live separately on either side of the glass, but there is a ramp that gives them both access to a landed area. Here they meet and mate although they spend the rest of their time apart, each in his or her half of the aquarium. The mating behavior varies greatly in the different species.

One final note: The presence of a male is not always necessary for reproduction. The females of many species (e.g., Diamondback Terrapins and Box Turtles) are able to store spermatozoa for up to four years and lay fertilized eggs even after such a prolonged separation from the male. It is not yet established whether all species have this ability.

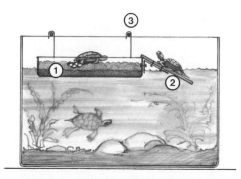

To lay its eggs in a layer of mixed sand and peat moss (1), the turtle climbs up a ramp (2) equipped with aluminum angle irons and affixed to the island. The island hangs from sticks (3) laid across the top of the aquarium.

## Incubation and Hatching of the Eggs

If our efforts have been rewarded with a successful mating there will soon be as many as eight eggs, sometimes even more. Both land and water turtles bury their eggs, and for the latter we have to suspend a dish filled with sand somewhere in the aquarium where the turtle can easily climb up on it. After the eggs are laid we carefully expose them, making sure that they stay in their original position. If they are turned over, the yolk crushes the embryo. It is best to mark the upper side of the eggs with a pencil (magic markers and ball-point pens contain poisons), number them, and record the weight and date of laying

# *Breeding Turtles*

of each egg. Fill a clear plastic box one third full with unfertilized, soaked, and then well squeezed peat moss; bury the eggs about two thirds deep in it; and place the cover over the container slightly ajar to allow for some ventilation. This method allows you to check on the eggs easily (see drawing on this page). For extra safety we place a hygrometer and a thermometer on a clean piece of paper on top of the peat in the container to check on the climate inside it. The humidity should be around 80% to 100%, and the temperature about 82°F (28°C). The proper temperature can be achieved by placing the incubating container over warm water (use an aquarium heater) or in a warm cellar (see drawing on this page).

Every four or five days the cover should be removed to allow the incubating chamber and the peat to air out. Be careful not to let water that has formed on the inside of the cover through condensation drip on the eggs. Tilt the cover and let the water drain into the incubator but not onto the eggs. As the embryos grow the eggs get heavier, as you will be able to tell if you weigh the eggs again after four to six weeks. Twelve to fifteen weeks will pass and sometimes as much as six months before the baby turtles hatch.

It sometimes happens that a turtle lays her eggs in the water. These are often not viable, but we should try to incubate them in any case. Only if the eggs show clearly visible cracks, the pores ooze a watery liquid that quickly solidifies, or a stench develops can we throw out the eggs in good conscience, not, however, without first cracking them and establishing whether or not they were fertile.

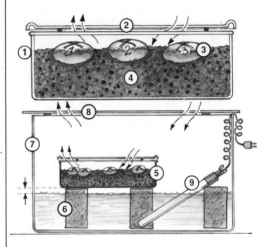

You can use as an incubator a clear plastic box (1), the cover of which has to have ventilating slits (2). The marked eggs (3) lie in a layer of peat moss (4). To maintain the proper climate for the incubator (5), place it on bricks (6) in a plastic aquarium (7) that has an almost air-tight glass cover (8). A heater with a thermostat (9) provides the temperature necessary for incubation.

# *Breeding Turtles*

## Raising the Young

After hatching, the young should stay in the incubator until the contents of the yolk bag, which is often still hanging more or less depleted from the plastron, are used up. The further raising of the young animals in a separate terrarium and on as varied a diet as possible usually presents no problems.

Ordinarily young turtles start eating two to three days — occasionally not until two to three weeks — after the yolk bag is gone. At first you should offer them fresh food every day, whether they are plant or meat eaters. Meat eaters have to grow somewhat older before you can increase the period between feedings. Just when and how this will happen has to be determined by careful observation. Depending on their appetites, young turtles will start passing feces five to ten days after the first feeding. The food should be chopped to fit the size of the mouth and carefully fortified with regular but not excessive doses of vitamins and minerals as well as calcium for proper development of the shell (page 46).

Soon after their birth we should start thinking seriously about selling or bartering the rapidly growing young animals unless we want to feed the whole voracious tribe for a year or two. (Or you may want to consider giving the animals away.) Start advertising in good time in aquarium and terrarium publications or in the newsletters of the groups listed on page 73. Keep in mind that neither summer vacation nor approaching winter is an opportune time for finding takers. The same is true if you advertise on bulletin boards in pet stores or in local papers. Sometimes animal shelters can help find interested people, but they are usually so overworked that they have little time to act as agents.

# Understanding Turtles

## Creatures Dating Back to the Beginnings of Our Earth

So far I have called your attention mainly to peculiarities of turtles that derive from their being untamed creatures, adversely affected by temperatures that are either too high or too low, by lack of space to move around in, by a monotonous diet, and by continual disruptions. In spite of these sensitivities, turtles belong to one of the few classes of animals that have survived from the great days of the dinosaurs to our time. The same can be said only of crocodiles and lizards. The turtles that still survive are, then, in a manner of speaking, witnesses of our earth's first days. Their ancestors roamed this earth 180 million years ago at a time when neither mammals nor birds as we know them today existed. Their origin goes back even farther to the period when the plants that we now unearth as coal were alive. These earliest turtles grew as large as 18 feet (6 m) and had much more highly rounded shells than the average modern turtle. When the reptiles — turtles among them — flourished, the climate in most areas of the earth was warm or even tropical, and most of today's turtles are still adapted to these conditions. Quite a few species, however, have adjusted to less inviting environments: hot and dry deserts, rocky slopes, and steppes. They have learned to survive in an inhospitable environment by falling into a sleeplike torpor during periods of cold, extreme heat, or drought and waking up refreshed when the surrounding conditions improve. But the inanimate forces of nature were not their only enemies. In the course of time, numerous predators (mammals and birds) arose against whom turtles had to defend themselves. They have been very successful at this, even when man the hunter made his appearance. Only the excessive exploitation of very recent times has brought many species to the verge of extinction. The worldwide decline of turtle populations has many causes: the manufacture of tortoise shell from the horny shields forming the shell of the Hawksbill Turtle; the popularity of turtle meat and turtle soup; the destruction of habitats, particularly that of the European Pond Turtle; and the collection and export of turtles for the pet trade, from which the Spur-tailed Mediterranean Land Tortoise has suffered especially. We should therefore feel a special obligation to appreciate our captive turtles and to create a congenial environment for them where they can live a long and happy life. For this we need above all to learn to read the animal's signals.

Unlike cats or dogs, turtles cannot communicate with us through facial expressions. Nor can they give voice to their feelings (except in some cases during mating). They suffer joy and pain silently. This can have grave consequences for animals under human care if the attendant misinterprets the signals inherent in the behavior of his charges. Many turtles have died a slow and agonizing death in front of their owners' eyes because of this lack of communication.

# *Understanding Turtles*

## How Sensitive Are Turtles

The turtle's solid shell easily creates the impression — a false impression, unfortunately — that the animal is immune to attack and completely imperturbable. Even its way of moving makes it appear easy-going and sluggish, at first glance, anyway. In fact turtles keep a watchful eye on their surroundings and react to any disturbance by hissing and retracting head and limbs quick as lightning. This response is a sign of fear and is meant to tell you that the turtle would prefer to be left alone. It would therefore be a mistake to keep peering at it and picking it up. For the sake of the well-being of the animal in your care, let me remind you once more that turtles are wild creatures and should be handled only when hygiene or the treatment of illness require it. Disruptions are upsetting to the animal and should be avoided whenever possible.

## Sensory Capacities

The turtle's shell is not made up of dead cells but is instead a live organ (page 62) capable, among other things, of picking up even the slightest vibrations of the ground that, to the animal in the wild, may signal the approach of predators. For us, this means that we should remove any source of constant vibration from the animal's vicinity. We should reduce the impact of vibrations from electric air pumps, filter motors, refrigerator compressors, pumps of oil heaters, etc. as much as possible.

The stand for the terrarium should not be in direct contact with a vibrating floor; its feet should rest on rubber or felt cushions.

**The Ears:** If turtles "hear" with their shells, what function do their ears have? Behind the eyes and the corners of the mouth, just where one would intuitively draw the ears, turtles do in fact have hearing organs, but without an external ear. The opening of the hearing canal is closed off by the tympanic membrane, a small oval that can be seen from the outside. Beneath this membrane, all the parts necessary for hearing are there, but opinions differ on the extent of a turtle's hearing capacities. A turtle's hearing seems to be limited to the lower frequencies — below those of our voices — such as those produced by the shaking of the ground. It goes without saying then that there is not much sense in calling the turtle's attention to food in the same high voice we use to call a cat. Drumming on the terrarium glass or using a clapper might produce more results in teaching the turtle tricks.

**Eyes and Nose:** Unlike hearing, the senses of sight and smell are very well developed in turtles. Turtles not only react quickly to optical stimuli but also recognize food by its smell from a long way off. In view of this we should avoid the continual stimulation of these senses and place the terrarium where the turtle will not constantly be startled by the appearance of people in its field of vision. We should also try not to expose the animal to strong smells, especially tobacco smoke.

A Narrow-bridged Mud Turtle *(Claudius angustatus)* in a threatening posture. This turtle, though only six inches (15 cm) long, is extremely aggressive.

## A Short Lesson in Turtle Anatomy

**The Shell:** As I have already mentioned, the shell is not a mass of dead cells. Its inner layers consist of bony plates that are at the same time parts of the spinal column, the ribs, the shoulder girdle, and membrane bones, so that it could be said of turtles both that they have grown attached to their shells and that their shells are part of their skeletons.

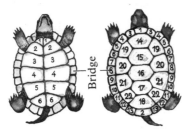

Scutes of the plastron: 1 gular, 2 humeral, 3 pectoral, 4 abdominal, 5 femoral, 6 anal. Scutes of the carapace: 1 nuchal, 2 supracaudal, 3–13 marginals, 14–18 centrals, 19–22 costals.

The bony part of the shell is covered with horny plates that expand and thicken as the turtle grows. This process results in "growth rings" which, however, are no accurate gauge of a turtle's age because they grow indistinct with age and eventually flake off.

The seams between these horny plates or scutes are sometimes covered by only a very thin horny skin that has grown with the most recent layer of the horny plates. The turtles are very sensitive to pressure in these areas.

Soft-shelled turtles lack the horny part of the shell and have a thick leathery skin instead.

The shell is the turtle's home and armor. The animal withdraws into it in different ways, depending on the species. The so-called hidden-necked turtles pull in the head completely and close off the opening with their often very scaly legs when they feel threatened. The tail can also be hidden by being flicked to one side so that the animal appears completely invulnerable.

The so-called side-necked turtles stow the head and neck sideways between the carapace and plastron. Their legs and tail generally lack a protective covering. Their defense seems less complete.

Some turtles not only retract the exposed parts of their anatomy but are

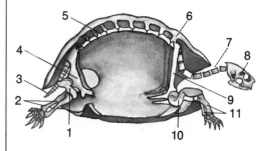

The turtle's shell is not an inanimate configuration but an integral part of the skeleton. The sketch shows the different elements of the skeleton: 1 upper leg, 2 lower leg, 3 tail vertebrae, 4 pelvic bone, 5 backbone, 6 vertebral plate, 7 neck vertebrae, 8 skull, 9 shoulder girdle, 10 upper arm, 11 lower arm.

Turtles in their native habitat. Above: The African Leopard Tortoise *(Testudo* [or *Geochelone] pardalis)* grows as large as 28 inches (70 cm) long. Below: The Diamond-back Terrapin, subspecies *Malaclemys terrapin centrata,* lives in the southeastern United States. The one pictured here is "on the alert" and ready to take flight.

able in addition to close off the openings tightly by drawing the lower shell, which is hinged in the middle, up against the rim of the carapace (Box turtle, page 18).

**"Beak" and Claws:** Not only the horny parts of the shell but also the sharp rim of the jaw (turtles lack teeth) and the claws on the feet keep growing continually. The horny growth of jaw and claws is not always apparent because the normal wear of biting hard foods and walking on rough surfaces keeps pace with it. With captive animals we have to watch out for overgrowth and take measures to correct it if necessary (page 50) because claws that are too long can get caught in cracks and a nail torn out can cause infection. Overgrown horny rims on the jaw interfere with eating.

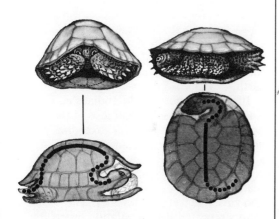

Hidden-necked turtles (left) draw their heads and arms back into the shell. Side-necked turtles (right) lay their heads sideways under the roof of the shell.

## The Body Language of Turtles

First of all we need to find out if our turtle forages for food during the day, at dusk, or perhaps at various hours of both day and night. Only when we are quite familiar with our turtle's pattern of activity can we judge whether its apathy merely indicates a phase of rest and is therefore normal or whether it represents the initial stage of an illness. Now we will have no problems interpreting the following types of behavior:

• The turtle is lying flat on the ground in natural or artificial sunlight with all four legs and the head stretched out full length: The turtle is taking a sunbath or lightbath.

• The turtle from a temperate zone is lying around in the terrarium more and more apathetically as fall approaches and refusing to eat: The animal is getting ready to hibernate.

• The turtle is pursuing its mate, trying to bite its head, neck, or feet. Many land turtles ram their shells into their mates, causing them to withdraw, and then mount them. Male aquatic turtles hover in the water above, below, or in front of their mates and tremble for several seconds with their forelegs outstretched (Red-eared Turtle and Cumberland Turtle), or bob up and down in the water, touching the bottom (*Clemmys* species): These are all courtship overtures. Courtship biting can easily result in superficial wounds that may bleed. It is up to the observer to decide if and when the injured animal should be separated from the aggressor. The animals should always

65

# Understanding Turtles

be separated if the bitten one is a weaker male. Such animals often serve as an outlet for frustrated sexual instincts.
• The turtles pace or swim along the glass wall restlessly or dig holes: This means either that something is wrong with the climate in the terrarium (too dry, too warm, or too humid) or that the turtle is looking for a place to deposit its eggs. Another possibility is that the turtle does not like the hiding place you have provided and is looking for a better one.

When sunbathing, turtles like to stretch all four limbs far out. Note that this animal has not been overfed.

## Giant Relatives

You will have a chance to watch many interesting and amusing incidents in the course of caring for your turtle over the years. This is particularly true if you keep more than one animal and they produce offspring in the terrarium. The lives of their larger cousins both on land and in the ocean are just as fascinating. Since you are unlikely to observe these armored giants in nature, I would like to tell you a little about the role turtles have played on this earth in the past and still play today.

## Turtles in Myth and History

Turtles occupy an almost godlike position in the myths of many peoples: The ancient Hindus pictured the world as a disk something like a plate that was supported by four elephants. These elephants were standing on the back of a huge turtle that was slowly moving through time.

Many North American Indians assigned a similar role to the turtle, seeing it as the foundation of the earth. According to their legends all creatures once lived on the back of a giant turtle that was adrift in the "primordial" sea. Later, crabs brought sand up from the bottom of the sea and mounded it on the turtle's shell until it turned into the earth.

Just how important the Indians considered the turtle is evident also in their notion that this animal was exceedingly wise and a friendly and shrewd source of advice.

As much as 300 years ago the amatory feats of sea turtles intrigued seafarers and gave rise to fantastic tales. The sailors reported that copulation lasted for two weeks without interruption, that the female then deposited her eggs and the sexual act was twice repeated, that the male was reduced to jelly inside and blinded by the exertion, and that the female had to carry him off on her back.

These are nothing more than sailor's yarns, but there is no need to turn to myths and fantastic tales for interesting and curious facts about turtles.

## The Giants of the Seychelles and the Galapagos Islands

Giant tortoises whose plastrons can reach a size of 44 to 48 inches (110–120 cm) still exist on the Seychelles and the Galapagos Archipelago. They survived there because the predatory mammals that brought about the extinction of their cousins on the mainland never reached those islands. There are reports that as little as three hundred years ago the Galapagos Islands were so heavily populated with tortoises that the whole landscape looked black. Travelers told that it was possible to walk long distances on the backs of the tortoises without touching the ground.

Things have changed a lot since that time. In the eighteenth and nineteenth century, first pirates, then whaling crews, and finally settlers came to the islands. All of them hunted and killed tortoises, not just to still their own hunger but also because the meat of these animals was considered a delicacy. Many claim that it is tastier and more tender than young poultry or veal.

What made tortoise meat especially attractive to seafaring people was how long the meat could be kept fresh. The huge animals were carried along across the seas in the holds of whaling boats up to a year and a half before they were slaughtered.

How could these poor creatures survive so long without dying of hunger or thirst? Like camels and many rodents living in the desert, the giant tortoises are able to store large amounts of fat in their bodies. When this fat is used up it supplies not only energy but also water. In the wild, this storage capacity allows the Galapagos tortoises to survive the dry seasons, although many cover great distances and climb considerable heights to get away from the arid coastal regions to the tropical inland forests where there is always plenty of water.

If we want to be accurate, we should not speak of "the" Galapagos tortoise because there are several races that differ from each other even in external appearance. The tortoises found on some islands, for instance, have rounded, dome-shaped carapaces, while the shells of their cousins on other islands are puckered up and gable-like, which gives the animals the freedom of movement necessary to feed on foliage they could not otherwise reach. Seeing these adaptations of body shape was one of the factors that inspired Darwin to develop his theories on the origin of species.

## Sea Turtles Going on Land

Apart from these and some other easily available facts, information about the biology of turtles is often difficult to gather. The Australian R. Bustard and the American A. Carr are among the few scientists who have studied the lives of

# Understanding Turtles

marine turtles extensively. What we know today about these creatures is based in large part on their work, and I, too, am indebted to it for much of what I am going to tell you about sea turtles.

Sea turtles are descended from terrestrial ancestors, but they have adapted perfectly to the aquatic life. One immediately apparent difference is that their carapaces, like those of fresh-water turtles, are much flatter and streamlined in shape than the highly arched backs of land species. This allows the animals to move through the water without encountering great resistance as they paddle with their large anterior flippers (really forearms with much elongated digital sections). The turtles can glide along slowly and elegantly or, if necessary, cut through the water at great speeds. They are much more clumsy on land where they often drag themselves laboriously across the sand of tropical beaches on their way to nest building sites. This pilgrimage takes place once a year during a period of about three months, and the nest building is almost always done in the evening or night hours. When the turtles have reached the right place each one digs a pit about two feet (60 cm) deep. Depending on the species, a turtle can deposit 500 to 1000 eggs in the course of several layings.

It is sometimes said that turtles weep when they lay their eggs; and it is true that thick, viscous tears start from their eyes. But these tears are not caused by labor pains. We know today that they are much saltier than human tears and that they are produced by glands with important functions. If the turtle could not cry, it would die of the excess sea salt it ingests with its food, salt that the kidneys alone cannot eliminate and that is therefore given off in the form of tears as well.

After laying its eggs the turtle covers the nest over with sand, and the only sign that remains of the nocturnal activity is a few tracks.

About two months later something happens that seemed inexplicable for a long time. In one single night and within a few minutes, all the hatchlings of one laying emerge simultaneously from the sand and make their way to the sea, literally covering the ground.

Many questions present themselves: Why do all the hatchlings come out of their eggs and later leave the nest at the same time? How do these creatures, buried in the sand and never having seen daylight, know when night has fallen above ground? How do they find their way to the sea they have never swum in?

We now know that the baby turtles cut a small hole in the soft leathery shell of the egg from the inside with the small, sharp, horny protrusion at the tip of their beak. Then they spend another day or so in their protective shell. This rest pause is important for the synchronization involved in the mass exist from the nesting pit, and it gives those who lag behind in their development a chance to cut through their egg shells. All the hatchlings wait together in the dark as

# Understanding Turtles

though anticipating a signal. And the signal is given: As soon as one hatchling starts moving and comes in contact with its neighbor, that one becomes active, nudges the next one in turn, and so on until the activity spreads all through the nest, which turns into a hive of crawling and digging bodies all striving upward. The uppermost animals scratch sand from the ceiling and pass it on to those below, and these keep on passing it down so that the entire group gradually makes its way toward the top. The digging can stop just as suddenly as it started, and it will stop just below the surface of the ground if the baby turtles reach the top in the daytime.

We can see the sense of this behavior. There are more predators on the lookout for food during the day, and the danger of being seen and eaten is considerably greater than during the night. But how do these newborn creatures know this?

During the first few hours of life the young turtles are not yet ready to survive in tropical conditions, and as soon as they penetrate to areas that are warmer than about 85°F (30°C) their digging will also cease and their immobility spread to their comrades working farther down. After sundown, when the earth gradually cools down again, the hatchlings will awaken to new life, burst from their nest, which often lies completely abandoned within one minute, and take off in the direction of the sea.

Just as these turtles are born with the ability to distinguish the cool night from the tropical day, they are also equipped with the instinct to move toward the place of greatest brightness. We can assume that on the natural beaches of these tropical regions the greatest brightness is created by the reflection of moon and stars on the surface of the water. Of course, even the cover of darkness does not offer complete protection. Some gulls forage for food at night and find an easy prey in the newborn turtles, as do the spider crabs. But traveling in a huge mass gives some individuals a chance to survive, because gulls and crabs can deal with only a fraction of the procession, and while they are busy eating, the rest of the turtles can reach the sea.

Here, too, hungry predators await them, and a considerable portion of the turtles ends up in the stomachs of fish. Their luckier fellows escape to the open waters. These then spend the next three to five years wandering with the currents, eating and growing until their time comes to swim to the shores where they were born and go through the nocturnal ritual of egg laying.

The more young turtles hatch at the same time, the greater their chance of reaching the open seas alive. The small sea turtles called Ridleys *(Lepidochelys olivacea)* have a special advantage in this respect because the parents go on land in groups. The females then lay their eggs, and the number of hatchlings emerging at the same time is proportionately larger. On the other hand, the chances of survival are small for turtles born on beaches where turtle eggs are harvested for human consumption. The number of hatchlings is likely to be so small that all the young turtles will fall victim to predators.

I have been able to tell you only a little bit about the events that take place in a sea turtle's life. Many aspects are still unknown to us and need to be explored to give us a fuller picture of these creatures that go back to the days of the dinosaurs. Let us hope that what we learn will be used at least in part for their benefit.

# Protected Turtle Species

The following table contains the names of those species of turtles which have been determined by the U.S. Fish and Wildlife Service to be endangered (E) or threatened (T). The list is updated annually and the information found on this page is as of 1982. The turtles listed may not be sold or traded without a special permit which is generally available only to zoos or other educational or research institutions.

| Common Species Name | Scientific Species Name | Historic Range | Status |
|---|---|---|---|
| Tartaruga | *Podocnemis expansa* | South America: Orinoco and Amazon River basins | E |
| Terrapin, River (=Tuntong) | *Batagur baska* | Malaysia, Bangladesh, Burma, India, Indonesia | E |
| Tomistoma | *Tomistoma schlegelii* | Malaysia, Indonesia | E |
| Tortoise, Angulated | *Geochelone yniphora* | Malagasy Republic (=Madagascar) | E |
| Tortoise, Bolson | *Gopherus flavomarginatus* | Mexico | E |
| Tortoise, Desert | *Gopherus agassizii* | U.S.A. (Utah, Arizona, California, Nevada); Mexico | T |
| Tortoise, Galapagos | *Geochelone elephantopus* | Ecuador (Galapagos Islands) | E |
| Tortoise, Indian Flap-shell | *Lissemys punctata punctata* | India, Pakistan, Bangladesh | E |
| Tortoise, Radiated | *Geochelone (=Testudo) radiata* | Malagasy Republic (=Madagascar) | E |
| Tracaja | *Podocnemis unfilis* | South America: Orinoco and Amazon River basins | E |
| Tuatara | *Sphenodon punctatus* | New Zealand | E |
| Turtle, Aquatic Box | *Terrapene coahuila* | Mexico | E |
| Turtle, Black Soft-shell | *Trionyx nigricans* | Bangladesh | E |
| Turtle, Burmese Peacock | *Morenia ocellata* | Burma | E |
| Turtle, Cuatro Cienegas Soft-shell | *Trionyx ater* | Mexico | E |
| Turtle, Geometric | *Geochelone geometrica* | Union of South Africa | T |

# Protected Turtle Species

| Common Species Name | Scientific Species Name | Historic Range | Status |
|---|---|---|---|
| Turtle, Green Sea | *Chelonia mydas* | Circumglobal in tropical and temperate seas and oceans | T |
| Turtle, Green Sea | *Chelonia mydas* | As above | E |
| Turtle, Hawksbill (= Carey) | *Eretmochelys imbricata* | Tropical seas | E |
| Turtle, Indian Sawback | *Kachuga tecta tecta* | India | E |
| Turtle, Indian Softshell | *Trionyx gangeticus* | Pakistan, India | E |
| Turtle, Kemp's (= Atlantic) Ridley Sea | *Lepidochelys kempii* | Tropical and temperate seas | E |
| Turtle, Leatherback Sea | *Dermochelys coriacea* | Tropical, temperate, and subpolar seas | E |
| Turtle, Loggerhead Sea | *Caretta caretta* | Circumglobal in tropical and temperate seas and oceans | T |
| Turtle, Olive (Pacific) Ridley Sea | *Lepidochelys olivacea* | As above | T |
| Turtle, Peacock Softshell | *Trionyx hurum* | India, Bangladesh | E |
| Turtle, Plymouth Red-bellied | *Chrysemys rubri-ventris bangsi* | U.S.A. (Massachusetts) | E |
| Turtle, Short-necked *or* Western Swamp | *Pseudemydura umbrina* | Australia | E |
| Turtle, Spotted Pond | *Geoclemmys (= Damonia) hamiltonii* | North India, Pakistan | E |
| Turtle, Three-keeled Asian | *Geomyda (= Nicoria) tricarinata* | Central India to Bangladesh and Burma | E |

# Books and Associations
# for Further Information

*Book of Turtles*
Richard E. Nicolls: Running Press

*Tortoises and Terrapins*
Saiga Publications

*Wonders of the Turtle World*
Wyatt Blassingame: Dodd

New York Turtle and Tortoise
Society
American Museum of Natural
History
New York, New York

Society of Amphibians and
Reptiles
Ohio

American Society of Ichthyology
and Herpetology
Smithsonian Institute
Washington, DC

# Index

74

# Index

# BARRON'S PREMIUM PET CARE SERIES

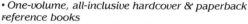

- One-volume, all-inclusive hardcover & paperback reference books
- Illustrated with from 80 to 300 stunning full-color photos, plus numerous drawings and charts.

**AQUARIUM FISH SURVIVAL MANUAL, THE** by Ward. A directory of more than 300 marine and freshwater fish species, including a guide to aquatic plants. 176 pp., 7³/₄" x 10", $19.95 NCR (5686-8) Hardcover.

**AUSTRALIAN FINCHES: THE COMPLETE BOOK OF** by Mobbs. An A-to-Z encyclopedia styled book, listing various finch species, cages, aviaries, flights, breeding etc. 144 pp., 8" x 11¹/₄", $18.95, NCR (6091-1) Hardcover.

**BEST PET NAME BOOK EVER, THE** by Eldridge. Presents 22 lists of names — 1500 in all to help give a pet the best name ever. 208 pp., 6¹⁵/₁₆" x 6¹⁵/₁₆", $5.95, Can. $7.95, (4258-1) Paperback.

**THE COMPLETE BOOK OF BUDGERIGARS** by B. Moizer & S. Moizer. The definitive reference on one of the world's most popular pets—Budgerigars (e.g. Parakeets). 144 pp., 8" x 11¹/₄", $16.95, NCR (6059-8) Hardcover.

**THE CAT CARE MANUAL** by Viner. Shows you how to meet all the needs of your cat and helps you understand its behavior. 160 pp., 7⁵/₈" x 9¹³/₁₆", $16.95, Can. $22.95 (5765-1) Hardcover.

**COMMUNICATING WITH YOUR DOG** by Baer. How to train your dog intelligently and humanely. 144 pp., 6¹/₂" x 7⁷/₈", $8.95, Can. $11.95 (4203-4) Paperback.

**COMPLETE BOOK OF DOG CARE, THE** by Klever. Dog-care expert answers questions about selecting, training, grooming and health care. 176 pp., 6⁵/₈" x 9¹/₄", $8.95, Can. $11.95 (4158-5) Paperback.

**THE DOG CARE MANUAL** by Alderton. Gives you expert pointers on the general and medical care of your dog, as well as on obedience training. 160 pp., 7⁵/₈" x 9¹³/₁₆", $16.95, Can. $22.95 (5764-3) Hardcover.

**GOLDFISH AND ORNAMENTAL CARP** by Penzes & Tölg. Covers everything from anatomy, biology and varieties to nutrition, "housing," and diseases. 136 pp., 7³/₄" x 10", $18.95, Can. $25.95 (5634-5) Hardcover.

**THE HORSE CARE MANUAL** by May. A veterinary surgeon covers all facets of horse and pony ownership, through a convenient question-and-answer format. 160 pp., 7¹/₂" x 9³/₄", $16.95, NCR (5795-3) Hardcover.

**LABYRINTH FISH** by Pinter. Teaches you about the feeding, breeding, and diseases of these fish, and about aquarium maintenance. 136 pp., 7³/₄" x 10", $18.95, Can. $25.95 (5635-3) Hardcover.

**NONVENOMOUS SNAKES** by Trutnau. Features detailed descriptions of over 100 snake species and covers feeding, breeding, illnesses, and terrariums. 192 pp., 7³/₄" x 10", $18.95, Can. $25.95 (5632-9) Hardcover.

**THE COMPLETE BOOK OF PARROTS** by Low. Everything that anyone needs to know about owning all kinds of parrots, as well as macaws, cockatoos, parakeets, and lorries. 144 pp., 7⁷/₈" x 11", $16.95, NCR (5971-9) Hardcover.

**WATER PLANTS IN THE AQUARIUM** by Scheurmann. Professional guidance in choosing the most suitable water plants for various types of aquariums and fish. 72 pp., 6¹/₂" x 7⁷/₈", $4.50, Can. $5.95 (3926-2) Paperback.

ISBN Prefix: 0-8120

**Barron's Educational Series, Inc.**
250 Wireless Boulevard, Hauppauge, New York 11788, For instant service call toll-free: 1-800-645-3476 In N. Y. call 1-800-257-5729.
In Canada: Georgetown Book Warehouse, 34 Armstrong Avenue, Georgetown, Ontario L7G 4R9. Sales: (416) 458-5506

Books can be purchased at your bookstore or directly from Barron's. Enclose check or money order for total amount plus sales tax where applicable and 10% for postage (minimum charge $1.50, Can. $2.00). All major credit cards are accepted. Prices subject to change without notice.